About the Editors

BILL FAWCETT has been a professor, teacher, corporate executive, and college dean. As a book packager for the last twenty years, Bill Fawcett & Associates has packaged over 250 titles for virtually every major publisher. Bill began his own novel writing with a juvenile series and then edited the eight-book Fleet series with David Drake, which has become a classic of military science fiction. He has collaborated on several novels, including mysteries such as the Authorized Mycroft Holmes mystery novels and the Madame Vernet Investigates series. Bill has edited or coedited over thirty anthologies, including *Hunters and Shooters* and *The Teams*, two oral histories of the Navy SEALs in Vietnam. He is also coeditor of *It Seemed Like a Good Idea*, the prequel to this volume.

BRIAN M. THOMSEN has been a publishing professional for close to twenty-five years. With over thirty short stories to his credit and numerous fiction anthologies, he is also the editor of such historical collections as *Shadows of Blue & Gray: The Civil War Writings of Ambrose Bierce, Commanding Voices of Blue & Gray, Blue & Gray at Sea,* and *The Man in the Arena: Selected Writings of Theodore Roosevelt,* as well as the critically acclaimed literary anthology *The American Fantasy Tradition.* He lives in Brooklyn with his loving wife, Donna, and two incredibly talented cats named Sparky and Minx.

You Did What?

You Did What?

Mad Plans and Great Historical Disasters

Edited by Bill Fawcett and Brian M. Thomsen

Perennial Currents

An Imprint of HarperCollins*Publishers*

HarperCollins books may be purchased for educational, business, or sales promotional use. For information please write: Special Markets Department, HarperCollins Publishers Inc., 10 East 53rd Street, New York, NY 10022.

FIRST EDITION

Designed by Elias Haslanger

Library of Congress Cataloging-in-Publication Data
You did what? : mad plans and great historical disasters / edited by Bill Fawcett and Brian Thomsen.
    p. cm.
    Includes index.
    ISBN 0-06-053250-5
      1. History—Miscellanea. I. Fawcett, Bill. II. Thomsen, Brian.

D10.Y73 2004
904—dc22

2003067585

04 05 06 07 08 ❖/RRD 10 9 8 7 6 5 4 3 2 1

Contents

INTRODUCTION

So many mistakes, so few pages. . . . This book should make you feel good, assuming you are not one of the powerful and famous. If you are rich and famous, get back to being important. This book is for the rest of us. It is for us to enjoy just how incredibly, amazingly, and spectacularly wrong those with great power can be. We have of course the advantage of 20/20 hindsight, though in many cases they really should have known better. One of the less publicized business-school rules of thumb is that a successful top executive is right about 45 percent of the time. The good ones pick the right 45 percent of the decisions to be right about. Makes you shudder to think what a failure's percentage is. Hmmm, that explains a lot about the government. But in some cases one or more decisions made by those who control the fate of others, often nations, has a totally unexpected (to Mr. Important at least) and often negative result.

So here is a collection of massive gaffes, really serious stupidities, and other similar bad mistakes made by those who were supposed to know better. It is perfectly acceptable to feel a bit superior to them as you read these pages. Being typical (read marginally impoverished and definitely not important) authors, those of us writing for this book share that feeling of second-guessed superiority, or at least share the amusement we all enjoy when someone important does a pratfall.

There were just as many really horrible decisions not covered in this book. For example, Louis XVI's decision to support the revolt of the British Colonies in America. This worked out well for what soon became the United States of America but not so well for him. The ideas fostered in the newly formed United States of America, or inspired by European philosophers, led directly to the French Revolution and cost Louis XVI his head, literally. Then there was the U.S. Army's decision to line up six divisions and have them watch from a few miles away an atomic bomb going off. Let's not forget the engineer who decided to use that nice, shiny, and flammable aluminum paint on the zeppelin *Hindenburg*. It also hurt to not include a few great ideas that were the cutting edge of past medical science: bleeding, phrenology, and skeletal diagnosis. But alas those must wait (are you listening, editor?) for yet another sequel. Perhaps the best and worst thing about doing books about other people's blunders is that it appears we will never run out of material. So here they are to entertain you with their most massive mistakes: the rich, the important, the famous, and the occasionally pompous. Enjoy.

You Did What?

You Kidnapped Whom?

It takes a lot of effort to make a series of mistakes so great that not only do they destroy your entire civilization but also become the stuff that makes one of the great epics of all times.

THE TERRIBLE CHOICES OF THE TROJAN WAR
TROY, THE BRONZE AGE

Brian M. Thomsen

Some of the greatest stories in history have their basis in a combination of actual events and legends, where the blurring of the line between the two creates a sense of truly epic storytelling and of heroes larger than life who are nonetheless men (centaurs and gods excluded, of course).

The factual history is unclear. Still, it took some pigheaded stupidity and shortsighted self-indulgence to effectively destroy the leading city of its day.

We know that indeed there was a city named Troy (also known as Ilium), believed to be located on a hill now called Hisarlik in the northwest reaches of Anatolia. However, this might not have been the location of the Troy as depicted in the chronicles of the Trojan War. Archaeological research has chosen a better candidate—namely, Troy VI, which was destroyed in 1270—given the following facts: there are records that show it was in contact with Greece during the hypothetical period of the conflict, Greece was a flourishing yet warlike civilization at the time, and it included as part of its realm Mycenae and other locales actually mentioned in the Homeric records (which is also mentioned in various contemporary corroborating Hittite records).

Thus, when it comes to the facts, we know that there was a city of Troy (which may or may not have been located where we thought it was) and that sometime during the classical age a war took place there, possibly over a dispute concerning control of trade through the Dardanelles.

But of course there is much more to the story. A lyrical chronicle of this great war based in mythology and reportage has been passed down by the great blind bard Homer in his epic ballads *The Iliad* and *The Odyssey*.

According to Homer, the Trojan War broke out when the Prince of Troy, Paris, abducted the wife of Menelaus of Sparta, the so-called Helen of Troy, whose face could launch a thousand ships.

Bad Idea #1: Never make off with the wife of a guy who has the pull to call on an entire army to get her back.

Menelaus persuaded his brother Agamemnon to amass an army against Troy to bring his wife back. This army included such great heroes as wily Odysseus, Nestor, and Achilles, whose inclusion as part of the martial force leads us to . . .

Bad Idea #2: Be careful what you choose; you will have to live (even after death) with the consequences.

According to legend and myth, the gods had offered Achilles (he of the legendary heel) a choice—he could live a long but ordinary life or he could live a short but heroic-unto-legend-worthy life. He chose the latter, and indeed acquitted himself exceptionally during the siege of Troy, and as a result died quite heroically in battle. It is accurate to note that he eventually had second thoughts on this choice as revealed in a passage of *The Odyssey,* where he is encountered in the Land of the Dead and pretty much admits his regrets.

Meanwhile, back at the war . . .

The battle rages for nine years as the Trojans had more than a few heroes of their own (such as Hector and his sons). Moreover, the city itself was well fortified with an enclosing wall that proved to be impenetrable from forces on the outside. As a result, after much hooting and hollering and laying to waste of the surrounding area, when all was said and done the Trojans and Helen were still safe and snug behind their city wall.

Moreover, they had gotten cocky.

•

Bad Idea #3: Watch whose advice you choose to ignore.

According to the myths the prophetess Cassandra was blessed with clairvoyant foresight and cursed with an aura that made those around her disbelieve anything she had to say.

Cassandra warned Hector and the Trojans that a plot to defeat Troy was afoot, and if it went forward, Troy would indeed fall.

They ignored her . . . and the expected disastrous results occurred.

The Greeks realized that they were getting nowhere so wily Odysseus decided that it was time to change tactics.

So one day the Trojans looked out on the enemy Greek camp, and lo and behold it was abandoned.

The Greeks had seemingly sailed away . . . but they had left something behind.

Bad Idea #4: Didn't the Trojans know to "Beware of Greeks bearing gifts"?

The Greeks had left behind a large wooden horse as a token of their esteem for so many years of good fighting; or, as said by sniveling Sinon, their left-behind spokesperson, "You won. We lost. Take this horse as the prize."

The Trojans dragged the horse into the city of Troy, inside her protective walls, which had so successfully withstood the Greeks.

Sure enough, night fell, a commando force dropped out of the horse and opened the gates from inside to allow in the now-returned Greek armies.

The Greeks won.

Troy fell.

But the story wasn't over yet.

Bad Idea #5: The gods hate a braggart so try not to piss them off.

Odysseus was quite pleased with himself that his plan had worked, and like the Trojans before him became too cocky—which is why it took him so long to get home (the delays of which are detailed in *The Odyssey*).

The gods had taken sides during the war and in some cases fought side by side with the mortal warriors.

Most of them did not appreciate having been bested by a mere mortal, even if he was Athena's favorite.

As to other victorious Greeks coming home from their victory . . .

Bad Idea #6: Never assume everything at home is hunky-dory after you have been away for close to ten years.

Agamemnon came home to the arms of his loving wife, who had been terribly lonely when he first had left so many years ago.
She got over it and took a lover.
Together they killed the returning war hero.

To recap
- Don't steal the wife of anyone with a big army.
- Dying a hero isn't all it's cracked up to be (at least according to a dead man).
- Don't ignore good advice or a well-advised warning.
- Beware of Greeks bearing gifts.
- Don't get cocky; the gods don't like it.
- And most important—never neglect your wife.

Even if the so-called Trojan War as we know it is mostly fanciful storytelling by a blind bard, it nonetheless illustrates many of the same lessons that are the real reasons we study history . . .
. . . namely, that there are those who learn from the mistakes of the past and those who don't and are destined to repeat them. These words, of course, being written in what is often called the New Rome, A.D. 2003.

You Insulted Whom?

Hell hath no fury as a woman scorned, and Rome managed to pick the wrong one to scorn more than once. But perhaps the most special case of this is that of Boudicca.

BOUDICCA AND THE ROMANS

BRITAIN, A.D. 43

Jody Lynn Nye

For a small and not very prosperous tribe like the Iceni, the Roman invasion of Britain in A.D. 43 must have appeared to be a good thing. The wealthy and powerful Belgic peoples, the Trinovantes and the Catuvellauni, who had invaded the island in 75 B.C. and conquered the lands to the south of their Norfolk territory, were constantly pushing their borders outward, occasionally threatening to envelop their neighbors. The Romans, at least, offered protected client status to those tribes who surrendered to them without a fight.

From A.D. 43 to 50 the Romans worked to develop the new province, establishing trade routes with ports at Camulodunum, Londinium and Richborough to bring in new goods to interest their British subjects in the fruits of the wider world. Prasutagus, king of one of the three tribes of the Iceni, welcomed Roman products and Roman philosophy. The Iceni started to feel comfortable in their new state. They struck their own silver coins, depicting the horses that were their greatest treasures, some of which went as tribute to their new overlords. For their part the Romans created a line of forts along the Fosse Way, a road that led from the southwest of the country northeast to the River Humber, to protect their conquered lands from the barbarians who lived outside their borders.

However, the Romans had not been accepted by everybody in Britain. The local peoples watched with trepidation as a *colonia* was established in Camulodunum (modern Colchester), a collection of villas around a trading center that would become home to soldiers who were retired from their legions but could be mustered again if needed. A huge temple to Claudius Caesar was raised there, built using funds raised not from donations of the faithful, as was customary, but by a levy on the captive kingdoms of Britain.

The Roman governor was constantly having to subdue revolts. One that was nearly successful was led by the great Celtic war leader Caractacus. The Romans became nervous about the other tribes in their conquered region, and invaded provinces beyond the original line of demarcation. They also announced to their client states a demand that all weapons except hunting implements be surrendered. Arms, especially beautifully made and ornamented iron swords crafted by skilled Celtic smiths, were prized by the Britons, who rebelled at having to give them up. Prasutagus, king of the Iceni, was the first to rise. He called upon his neighbors to the south to join him. The Romans put down this minor revolt, yet left Prasutagus and his fellow rulers as kings.

The tribes came to understand that their conquerors did not entirely trust them. They were wise enough to know that a lack of trust could easily give way to fear. They prepared to defend their interests against their overlords but remained outwardly pro-

Roman, paying the hated taxes in exchange for the benefits of citizenship.

In A.D. 60, Prasutagus died, leaving his kingdom jointly in the hands of his two daughters and Emperor Nero, in hopes that the friendly relationship with Rome would persist after his death. The local imperial agents, seeing an opportunity to destroy the royal family, invaded the Iceni state, looted the residence, and raped the two princesses in the presence of their mother, Queen Boudicca, who was flogged by slaves. The Roman agents hoped the humiliation of the royal house would drive the Iceni to their knees, so they could stop pretending that these British barbarians were equal to civilized Romans. It was a terrible mistake. They did not understand the will of Boudicca.

Furious and insulted, the queen plotted revolution with surrounding tribes. She was reputed to be a great beauty, but she must have had charisma and a strong mind as well. She managed to convince the others that their only hope lay in driving the Romans out. In A.D. 60, the Iceni, accompanied by the Trinovantes and many others, rose in revolt against the occupiers. Their prized horses drew armed warriors in lightly built woven chariots, not the scythe-wheeled carts that are often depicted in movies. Boudicca herself led her force southward.

Their first target was the *colonia* at Camulodunum. Most of the settlers fled to the despised temple and sent for help from the governor, Suetonius. Suetonius was in the northwest, battling the druids in Anglesey. They also sent messages to the agent in Londinium, Catus Decianus, who misunderstood the scope of the invasion. He sent only two hundred men, most of whom were killed by the mob of Britons, along with the hapless townsfolk. The temple in which the settlers made their last stand was destroyed to its foundations. The town was burned. Even the cemetery was desecrated.

Boudicca's army moved southward, fighting and burning as it went. It met the Ninth Roman Legion outside of Longthorpe in Cambridgeshire, and killed every man but the mounted cavalry, who escaped to sound the alarm. Suetonius at last understood the seriousness of the situation. He rushed to defeat the druids and moved his two legions, the Fourteenth and the Twentieth, back toward Londinium.

In the meantime, Boudicca's force was growing. It rolled over Londinium, burning it to the ground. As many Romans who could flee did, including Decianus, the agent for Londinium. They were wise to leave. Others who could not or would not flee almost all died. Historians claim as many as 70,000 Romans and Roman sympathizers were killed. Some contemporary accounts tell of atrocities committed by the rebel army out of anger and frustration. Neither women nor children were spared hideous deaths.

Once she had destroyed Londinium, Boudicca turned her force northward along Watling Street, the great Roman road that led northwest, in pursuit of Suetonius and his army, hoping to throw the Romans out of Britain once and for all. She had little choice but to try; word had spread of the revolt. Soon other legions would cross the channel to support the beleaguered governor. Other risings were taking place across Britain as news of Boudicca's defeat of Camulodunum and Londinium became known. If she could defeat Suetonius now, the Romans might withdraw, putting aside Britain as too expensive a province to maintain, both in lives and in money.

The Iceni-led force, now over 100,000 strong, caught up with the Romans near the junction of Watling Street and the Fosse Way, east of the River Anker near Manduessedum. From the beginning it was a good choice of battlefield—for the Romans. They were perched on a wooded bluff cut by deep ravines, with more woods behind them, and a wide-open plain facing their enemies, who needed to cross the river to reach them. At the northwest end of the legions' line was a military base that they could use for defense if necessary. Suetonius had time to wait for reinforcements from along the Fosse Way. Though they probably totaled fewer than 15,000 men, the Romans had time to organize themselves and wait for the juggernaut to descend.

Boudica was brave to the end. She is reported to have given her troops a pep talk, taunting them by saying, "Win the battle or perish; that is what I, a woman, will do; you men can live on in slavery if that is what you want."

Unfortunately, perish they did. The disorganization of the enormous mob, some say numbering as many as 250,000 men, women, and children, caused them to get in one another's way. Because of the crowding their long swords were useless. Those who were not killed by the volley of Roman javelins at the start of the battle were probably hacked to death by Roman short swords. The Iceni and Trinovantes were so convinced they would win that they allowed women and children to sit on carts around the battlefield like spectators at a ball game. Those helpless ones, too, were killed by the legionaries. Even pack animals were slaughtered. When the battle ended, 80,000 Britons were dead, but only 400 Romans.

Legend has Boudicca falling on her sword to avoid capture, but a historian of the time, Dio, claims that she poisoned herself. In any case, she was never taken prisoner by the Romans.

Today, no one recalls the names of the Roman agents who humiliated Boudicca and caused the bloody uprising, but a statue of the Iceni queen in her chariot stands in London to memorialize her struggle against the foreign invaders.

You Invited Whom?

When you have the most to lose, mistakes have a way of getting out of hand. And too often, even today, the politicians take the easy way out. But sometimes the faster, less expensive solution is not really a good idea.

ANCIENT ROME AND THE BARBARIANS

EMPEROR VALERIAN

ROME, A.D. 300

E. J. Neiburger

In the second, third and fourth centuries, Rome was the greatest power in the world. This far-flung empire included Europe, the British Isles, North Africa, the Middle East and even parts of Asia. Such a massive empire, with thousands of miles of frontier borders, required efficient organizational bureaucracies, immense armies and enormous tax revenues to maintain stability. Opposing Rome (inside and out) were millions of people in small disorganized tribes and petty kingdoms who generally were no match for the Roman military, its gold and silver and its sophisticated diplomats.

Around A.D. 100, European "barbarians" (as the Roman's called them) began to increase in population, forming large villages. These groups often merged into confederacies and, though often quarreling, cooperated in joint military actions against their neighbors, including Rome. Often one group would displace another tribe, which would force a weaker neighbor into the territory of another in a falling domino–type effect. When directed against Roman territory, these attacks were often easily repulsed by the Roman military, especially during good economic times. But when economic and environmental hardships or internal politics weakened the Roman tax base or political resolve, Rome lost territory to the barbarians.

To halt these losses, Rome often hired barbarian armies to act as buffers from these attacks. This policy, though occasionally used in the past, was begun in earnest by Rome's worst military leader, the ill-fated emperor Valerian (who was captured by the Pesians in A.D. 260). The theory behind this policy was logical. Let the barbarians kill off each other. The more that die, the weaker they get and the fewer individuals that must be paid, be it enemy or friend. In many cases, if the barbarian mercenaries were victorious but weakened, Roman soldiers could kill them after the battle and thus save all that money. The logic was good though perhaps more than a tad unethical. Unfortunately the barbarians thought the same way about the Romans. Such a time occurred in the middle of the third century when a Roman army was defeated by Persia and Rome lost Dacia (modern day Romania) to invaders.

In A.D. 260, Roman soldiers, retreating from military disasters with Persia, allowed the Alamanni tribe to occupy the Upper Danube and Rhine territories as a paid buffer state. With more territory than its 400,000 soldiers could effectively patrol, Rome decided to use barbarians to insulate it from its enemies. The Alamanni soon quarreled among themselves, splitting into two separate tribes, the Visigoths and Ostrogoths.

By A.D. 330, Rome had divided into two separate empires, centered in Rome (West) and Constantinople (East). The Roman armies and their allies were thinly strung along the frontiers with large mobile field armies held in reserve to plug "holes" by periodic attackers. This operated efficiently for point attacks but failed to stem the tide of large, broadscale attacks over wide areas of their borders. Such broad attacks effected by confederacies of barbarian tribes were increasing. To fill the gaps, barbarian armies from the Franks, Alamanni, Goths, Vandals, Quadi, Marcomanni, Heruli, Alans, Lombards, Jutes, Angles, Saxons and Huns were hired and paid with money and land. They protected Rome at times, but attacked it at others. Rome had no other choice. They needed more soldiers and their citizens were willing to pay (sometimes not) but would not serve.

The use of barbarian troops caused a deep suspicion and distrust among the Romans, who needed the protection of barbarian armies but didn't like them and strongly objected to the high taxes imposed upon them by their emperors to pay these unruly, smelly soldiers. Barbarians were neither trustworthy nor loyal, especially when their pay was overdue (not to mention frequent Roman lies, double-crosses and assassinations).

Occasionally this ill will boiled over into action, such as the A.D. 378 "preventative" massacre of barbarian Goths employed in the Roman army (and their families) by Constantinople Romans after a military defeat by an opposing barbarian army. Other massacres of "Roman" barbarian soldiers occurred in A.D. 390 and A.D. 408. Because of these actions, monetary "disagreements" and the general "we-are-better-than-you-scum" attitude of the Romans, the barbarians did not entirely trust their Roman "friends."

Often the barbarians became Romans themselves and held

high office. Fraomer, king of the Alamanni, was a Roman officer in
A.D. 372. The Frank Bauto and Vandal Stilicho were barbarian generals who at one time actually ruled Rome. The desire was to possess what the Romans had—security, land, power, wealth, culture
and fame—simple desires expressed by most barbarians (and
Romans too). Around A.D. 370, the Chinese army uprooted the
pesky Huns, driving them west into the Middle East and Europe.
In A.D. 390 the Huns joined the Alans and attacked the Ostrogoths,
who were then pushed into Visigoth land. After the battle of
Dniester, the 200,000 surviving but defeated Visigoths begged to
be admitted to Roman territory. After first being refused and then
poorly treated, the Visigoths overwhelmed the small garrisons of
Roman soldiers and "peacefully" flooded into Roman territory
(Moesia). Badly outnumbered and taking the hint, the Roman
frontier troops were evacuated, only to be attacked by the out-
flanking Huns, who circled in from the north. They avoided anni-
hilation only by paying the Huns a large inducement of silver.

Who did this? It becomes a parade of emperors—Caesars, that
is—who found it convenient or necessary to use the barbarians,
beginning with Valetinian, an Italian Roman, and ending with
Alaric, who was most definitely not a Roman. By the late fourth
century, barbarian armies were embroiled as mercenaries in the
incessant Roman civil wars of that period. In A.D. 383, Roman general Magnus moved from Britain to Gaul, using paid German barbarian troops to retake central Europe and put himself on the
throne. Emperor Valentinian used Franks, Huns and Alans to stop
the general. In A.D. 387, Maximus deposed Valentinian as emperor
of the Western Empire. The Eastern Empire emperor, Theodosius,
hired a Visigoth army to kill Maximus and restore Valentinian to

the Western Empire throne, which they accomplished in A.D. 392. After restoration, neither emperor could adequately pay off their barbarian troops, who then collected their pay by sacking all of Macedonia. Unfortunately for the Romans, Valentinian died the next year (bad luck) and the Frank king, Arbogastes, declared his man, Eugenius, emperor of the West. In A.D. 394, an army of 20,000 Visigoths attacked the Western Empire armies and murdered the Frank-controlled Eugenius (more bad luck). They declared Theodosius as emperor of both East and West Roman Empires. A few months later, Theodosius died of natural causes (a rarity in Roman politics). Vandal general Stilicho then took the throne of the Western Empire. The emperor of Rome was a barbarian.

The general attacked a Visigoth army commanded by Alaric I, which was invading northern Italy in A.D. 397. He also planned a counterattack on the Eastern Empire, which had secretly funded Alaric. After several years of inconclusive battles, Alaric was driven north, out of Italy, by a combination of a Hun army hired by Rome and attacks on his northern flank by his "brother barbarians," the Vandals, Suebi and Alans. An A.D. 407 revolt by Romans stationed in Britain (no pay) brought Constantine into Europe as a new self-declared Western emperor. There were three individuals now claiming the Western Empire throne; four individuals claiming its wealth. A deal was struck between Emperor Constantine in Gaul, Emperor Stilicho in Rome, Emperor Honorius in Ravinia and General Alaric (no claim on the throne . . . just all the money) in northern Italy to leave Rome alone and, instead, attack the Balkans. Each party had their own barbarian troops. The deal fell through when Rome could not pay Alaric the enormous fee he demanded (after a wild-goose chase to Epirus in the Balkans), so in true barbarian fashion, his Visigoths blockaded Rome, held it for ransom and, when no one paid, sacked it in A.D. 410. Alaric died of natural causes (bad luck) a few months later while seeking food for his troops in southern Italy.

After the initial sacking, attacks on Rome became more commonplace. Constantine fought a number of battles against the Vandals, Suebi and Alans using Frank and Alamanni troops. He won some, lost some and was eventually destroyed by Emperor Honorius's barbarian mercenaries . . . including Alaric's brother, Athaulf, who was given the province of Aquitaine (central France) and most of Gaul as payment for his assistance. Innumerable battles were fought between local barbarians over land, payments and assassinations. In the middle of the fifth century, Attila the Hun appeared on the scene. He and his brother Bleda ravaged Asia and the Middle East. They were paid off by Constantinople, and after a brief fallout (in which Attila murdered Bleda) entered Europe, where the Huns were defeated in France by Aetius and his Gaul and Visigoth army. Attila retreated to Hungary and then moved south into Italy. In A.D. 452 the Huns were at the gates of Rome but stopped short of sacking the city. There is mention of a payoff as well as a malaria epidemic, which caused Attila (the unlucky) to withdraw to Hungary, where he died in A.D. 453. The Huns separated into small groups and hired out their services to the highest bidder. Barbarian "protectors" and their allies sacked Rome twice in later years.

The following year Eastern emperor Valentinian had Aetius killed but was not wealthy enough to afford the barbarian armies that would ensure control of his empire. Europe was carved up by the barbarians, and by A.D. 510 the last puppet Roman emperor

(West), Romulus Augustulus, died peacefully in retirement while his "hired" Skirian barbarians ruled Rome.

During the first through fifth centuries, barbarians attacked and defended territory that included Italy. The Romans hired barbarians to keep them safe. It was these same barbarians who became the "new" Romans and then, in turn, were destroyed and replaced by other barbarians. Money and luck ruled the day for a while. Then the Italian Romans learned that lesson about a free lunch. As these Roman emperors too often found out, sometimes you don't always get what you pay for.

YOUR SON DID WHAT?

You can pick your friends and avoid your enemies, but family you are stuck with. Then comes the problem of when your family is your enemy, or maybe your friend. Worse yet, sometimes when you get to pick your family, it does not work out so well.

HENRY, ELEANOR, AND THEIR ROYAL BROOD
ENGLAND, TWELFTH CENTURY

Brian M. Thomsen

King Henry II (1133–1189) was the first of the Plantagenets (the son of Geoffrey Plantagenet and Matilda, the daughter of Henry I). He ascended to the throne of England (more precisely, wrested it away from the control of King Stephen) in 1154 amid an era of chaos, anarchy and petty squabbling that had weakened Britain in terms of empire and infrastructure. Within a few short (albeit bloody) years he had established a competent and self-sufficient bureaucracy of state as well as an enforced hold/rule of the lesser barons and rulers, who had always been involved in various landgrabs and feuds under the administration (or more precisely, lack thereof) of his predecessor.

Indeed, with the inclusion of the holdings that he inherited upon his father's death in 1151 (Normandy and Anjou, the province of his birth) and his marriage to Eleanor of Aquitaine (ex-wife of King Louis VII of France) in 1152, and the other lands he acquired through conquest of disputed territories in the British Isles, Henry II was well on his way to establishing England as a world power. (Even though technically his French holdings were as a vassal subservient to the king of France, their breadth in conjunction with the holdings on the British Isles placed him in a position of marked superiority to the French crown—a matter of not insubstantial discord for years to come.)

Henry II approached his empire as a business. He reformed feudalism to centralize his own power base, razed unauthorized manors and fortresses that might house sites of future rebellion, reformed the courts and revitalized the exchequer by replacing the lower noble appointees with government clerks and bureaucrats, whose sole responsibility was in seeing that his (Henry II's) instructions were followed and that the Crown was given its due from every transaction. Henry II further undercut the noble appointees by centralizing and standardizing laws and the courts, replacing disparate traditions such as trial by ordeal with the right to a jury trial, thus dissipating the barons' and lords' ability to rule by whim.

Thus in matters of state and diplomacy, Henry II had proven himself a master, partly due to his willingness to make hard and daring choices and his shrewdness in judging the character of subordinates, thus enabling him to succeed in picking the right and most trustworthy person for a given position.

Unfortunately it cannot be said that he showed similar mastery in matters of hearth and family.

His marriage to Eleanor of Aquitaine, though at the time politically and financially rewarding, was nonetheless a match made for the divorce courts. Whether or not she rode bare-breasted into the Holy Land during the Crusades, as alleged by some, she was no doubt brazen and rebellious and used to being the mistress of her own fate. In many ways she considered herself more than Henry II's equal (she was indeed a queen before he was a king, after all), and as a result was frequently at odds with the decisions that her husband made, particularly those that would strengthen England's hand over France's.

The unrest caused by the queen's opposition to the king and her obvious divided loyalties to the empire eventually led to her exile-in-state/imprisonment, which though it contained her influence did little to quell the long-term difficulties to Henry II's reign. She had already instilled her views and opinions on their offspring, who would eventually succeed Henry II to the throne and were actively engaged in accelerating that succession to a date prior to their father's actual passing from the mortal realm.

There was of course the usual amount of sibling rivalry, which was cut in two by the early demises of sons Henry and Geoffrey, who might have indeed been the smartest of the brood, and had they survived might have indeed preserved their father's legacy . . . but they didn't, and Henry II was left to contend with their brothers (his sons).

Richard (the so-called Lionhearted) had all of the outward appearances of a strong leader and was rumored to be his mother's favorite because of his ties to France, but he was more interested in the Crusades and being "at wars" than attending to matters of state or indeed even learning such matters from his father, who had proven himself a master. Whether it was because he saw the role of king differently than his father or whether it was just that he was in his mother's thrall, Richard soon evolved into one of Henry II's principal rivals for the throne.

John, on the other hand, was Henry II's favorite of the surviving sons, but he too resisted learning the lessons of state at his father's knee. For the most part John was lazy and reminiscent of the anarchic nobles that his father had managed to wrestle out of power during his ascendancy to the throne. By supporting Richard in his rebellion against Henry II, John saw that he had secured for himself the best of both worlds—the unseating of Henry in favor of Richard, who would then spend most of his time waging war somewhere, thus allowing himself all of the benefits of the crown without any of the responsibilities.

As a result, Richard attacked and unseated Henry II on July 4, 1189, with the help of his brother, John, and Phillip II of France. He became king and Henry II died two days later, and immediately thereafter the empire that Henry II had constructed began to unravel.

The two brothers quarreled much in the same manner that they had with their now-deceased father, and their aforementioned proclivities (Richard's love of war abroad and John's selfishness) loosened the controls that the throne had over the royals. Moreover, neither brother had acquired any skill at politics or negotiation and often fell back on military might rather than actually solving the problem at hand. This situation was further aggravated after Richard's death when John ascended to the throne and immediately ran afoul of Richard's greatest ally, Phillip of France, the pope and his own royal court. He lost most of the family lands in France and then tried to raise the money to wage a war to reclaim them by raising taxes, while groveling back to Rome to regain papal favor.

The capital was raised, much to the nobles' chagrin, and the war was waged, but the outcome was far from successful, leaving England defeated and disheartened. Moreover, the now nonvictorious King John was facing a rebellion at home by the very same nobles he had taxed and neglected, and as a result he was forced to sign the Magna Carta, which basically reinstated the anarchic rights of the nobles that had been put under control by Henry II.

Thus in less than a generation all of the great strides that Henry II had accomplished for England were undone by his sons. Had the first Plantagenet spent as much time and attention on his heirs as he had on his job as king, his success might have been longer lasting.

You Arrested Whom?

Hundreds of years ago two very different men rose to power in what was the primary arena of strength in their time, the arena of faith and religion.

POPE NICHOLAS III

ROME, A.D. 1244

Edward E. Kramer

The Magna Carta is often thought of as the cornerstone of liberty and the chief defense against arbitrary and unjust rule in England. Signed by King John in 1215, it also limited the claims of Jewish moneylenders, protecting the English barons, who had never intended to repay the loans. Pope Innocent III also issued a decree that forced Jews to wear a badge or a hat as a means of segregating them from other peoples in the land. Jews who did not cooperate were subjected to fines and incarceration—every aspect of their lives was controlled.

It was also the year that Giovanni Gaetano Orsini was born to Perna Gaetana Gaetani, the newest member of one of the oldest famililes in the history of Rome. Giovanni's father was Senator Matteo Rosso Orsini, of the historic Roman family of Popes Paul I and Eugenius II. In his elected role, Matteo had opposed Emperor Frederick II, siding with Pope Gregory IX, saving the city of Rome for the Guelfic cause. He became good friends with St. Francis of Assisi, founder of the Franciscans, whose favor from the Order was later rewarded by Matteo's son, Giovanni, in his position as both cardinal and pope.

In 1240 C.E., the king of France ordered that a public disputation take place between Nicholas Donin, a Christian apologist, and Rabbi Yehiel of Paris; the public debate was held for the purpose of degrading Jewish religion and converting Jews. In the end, Pope Gregory IX declared the Christian theologian the winner, and the Jewish Talmud was declared an evil work. As a result, the pope issued a bull for the burning of the Talmud everywhere, and to establish inquisitions and censors over other Jewish writings.

Abulafia was also born in 1240 in Saragossa, Spain. His father, an eccentric adventurer from Saragossa, taught him the Torah and Talmud at a very early age. When Abulafia was eighteen years old, his father died. Like his late father, he immediately set off on a career of travel and learning. Abulafia studied the sciences, philosophy, logic, medicine, and many other subjects. He went to the Holy Land but could get no farther than Acre due to the Crusades.

Pope Innocent IV, grateful for the services rendered by Rosso, promoted Giovanni Orsini to cardinal-deacon in 1244, with the title of St. Nicholas, in Carcere Tulliano. So great was Giovanni's influence in the Sacred College that the election of Urban IV was mainly due to his intervention. Urban named him general inquisitor and protector of the Franciscans. Later he played a prominent part at the elections of Gregory X, who received the tiara at his hands, and of John XXI, whose counselor he became and who named him archpriest of St. Peter's. After a period when there was no pope for six months, he succeeded John as Pope Nicholas III.

When Abulafia traveled in Spain and Italy, he came into contact with the spreading influence of Jewish mysticism called Kabbalah, a part of the Hebrew Scriptures that describes creation and God's relationship to that creation. It defines both a series of texts, particularly the *Zohar, Bahir,* and the *Sefer Yetzirah,* as well as defining a system of mysticism and interpretation of Scripture. It also consists of meditative, devotional, mystical and magical practices, which were taught only to a select few. Some aspects of Kabbalah have also been studied and used by non-Jews for hundreds of years.

The most influential Kabbalistic document, the *Sefer ha-Zohar,* or "Book of Splendor," was written by Rabbi Shimon Bar Yochai at about 150 C.E. It contains a series of separate scriptures covering a wide range of subjects, from a verse-by-verse commentary on the Torah to highly theosophical descriptions of processes within God. It describes the 125 levels man can achieve, including the highest level, "Eliyahu the Prophet," where the prophet himself is said to come.

But the existing Kabbalistic works did not fully satisfy him. Abulafia began composing a new book that would be closer to what he called the "real truth." Through his lectures, he gained a small following among the less educated and more superstitious Jews of Spain. Many rabbis opposed his new form of Kaballah and forced him to leave for Italy. In 1271, he wrote that God granted him a vision and he received the spirit of prophecy.

From then on, Abulafia called himself Raziel, "the seer of God's secrets." In one of his more popular apocalyptic pamphlets, he wrote:

> The Lord's spirit reached my mouth and worked through me so that I manifested many dread and awful sights with signs and wonders. When I reached to the Names and untied the seal bands, the Lord of all revealed Himself to

me, and made known to me His secret, and informed me
concerning the end of the exile and the beginning of the
redemption.

In one of Pope Nicholas III (Giovanni)'s decrees, he wrote that
one hundred and fifty Jews must hear conversion sermons in Rome
every week. In another, he claimed to be "Vicar of God," which would
be the same as calling himself "another God." The term "antichrist,"
incidentally, is translated from the Greek *vicarius christi*, or "Vicar of
Christ." He is best known, however, in literature, when Dante
Alighieri placed him in the Third Circle of Hell (Canto 19), for those
guilty of simony—buying and selling the grace of God.

Abulafia's own writings tell us it was then that God had
ordered him to go to Rome. His divine mission, in response to
Nicholas's actions, was to convert the pope to Judaism and invoke
his assistance to bring the Jews home to the Holy Land—still occupied by the Christian Crusaders. His students pled with him not to
go, but after a second vision Abulafia learned that he was the Son
of God, and was urged to visit Nicholas III.

In a letter, Abulafia told the pope that he dreamed of dissolving
the differences between Judaism, Christianity and Islam, and
wished to meet with Nicholas III to discuss his ideas and ease the
suffering of the Jews. On Rosh Hashanah, in 1280 C.E., Abulafia set
out to Rome. Word spread quickly about the proposed meeting,
and the irate pope immediately erected a stake—Nicholas III
ordered Abulafia's execution upon arrival.

When the mystic arrived in Rome, he discovered that the pope
had gone to the castle of Sorriano near Viterbo. As he reached the
papal residency, Abulafia was immediately arrested and incarcerated.

Despite his apparently inevitable demise, he told followers not to worry. Many of the soldiers, however, did. Abulafia's reputation in Kabbalah had long ago come to the attention of the pope, which was probably why Nicholas III was absent as the rabbi approached.

Abraham Abulafia was never executed. He timed his trip exactly to a date specified in the *Zohar* written over a thousand years earlier:

> And on the sixth day [Friday] on the twenty-fifth day of the sixth month the star will appear and be gathered to the seventh day [the Sabbath]. And after seventy days, it will be covered up and will be seen no more. On the first day it will be visible in the city of Rome, and on that day three high walls of the city of Rome will fall, and the great palace there will collapse and the ruler of that city will die.

Pope Nicholas III suddenly died of a heart attack on August 22, 1280, which fell on the twenty-fifth day of Elul, the sixth month counting from Nissan. This date agrees with the *Zohar* regarding the demise of the ruler of Rome. Abulafia was released from jail, but even the Jewish communities of Italy were afraid to help him, as the new pope was likely to believe that Abulafia had killed the pope. The congruency between the predicted date of the death of the Roman ruler according to the *Zohar* and the death of Nicholas III remains far from coincidental.

Was it the magic of the Kaballah? Does it matter? Pope Nicholas III set a record for really bad theological and social decisions. Quite a distinction for anyone to achieve.

You Armed Whom?

Give a hungry man a fish and he eats; give him a fishing pole and he eats many times. Give him a weapon and he may get very cranky. In this case you had to wonder just what the cardinal was thinking. Or rather if he was thinking at all.

THE CRUSADE THAT RAN AMOK

HUNGARY, 1514

Bill Fawcett

It had been almost three hundred years since the Crusades to the Holy Land had ended in complete failure—long enough for both the horrible suffering and the lack of success to be forgotten and the myth of the Holy Crusades to be remembered. At this time Hungary was one of the leading powers of Christianity. It had been the first line of defense in the Balkans since Constantinople fell. The cardinal in charge of Hungary, Thomas Bakocz, was faced with a dilemma. The Turkish empire, and with it Islam, was growing in strength. For years Bakocz had encouraged the Hungarian nobility to take direct action against the Turks, but there had been very little interest in such a high-risk endeavor when the Turks were not directly threatening the nobles he approached.

So what was the cardinal to do? He saw, perhaps with great insight, that the continuing growth in Turkish strength promised disaster for Christian Hungary. The time to act was now, while

Hungary was still strong. Something had to be done. And there was something. It had been centuries since a crusade had been declared against infidels. There had been a few against Christian heretics. Heretics were often seen as a greater threat than infidels by the church. Cardinal Bakocz would declare a crusade. If the nobles wouldn't fight, then he'd call on the mass of serfs who suffered virtual enslavement on the Hungarian nobles' estates.

The response to a papal bull declaring the crusade against the Turks published on April 16, 1514, was beyond even the cardinal's greatest hopes. Life as a serf in sixteenth-century Hungary went from miserable and dreary to much worse. A serf who tried to leave the estate was often hunted down and both he and his family tortured. Free only on paper—and most serfs couldn't read—the serf was a virtual slave unless he left to do the work of the Lord. So in answer to a call for a crusade, any serf could safely leave the drudgery of the land he was bound to and even be guaranteed heaven as a side benefit. There was probably not a lot of debate in any serf's mind on what to do. Within a few months over 100,000 serfs had gathered in answer to the cardinal's call. They even had an experienced and proven leader, Gyorgy Dozsa. Dozsa was a Transylvanian nobleman and what passed for what we call today a liberal. He not only had commanded armies before but was personally sympathetic to the situation of the serf.

There was only one problem with the crusade. The king of Hungary had just concluded at about the same time a wide-ranging peace and trade accord with the Turks. And with a sizable percentage of the healthiest serfs in the army rather than working the fields, the crops were going untended and famine, not to mention the nobles' possible poverty, was likely. Pressure was brought on the cardinal and the pope to rescind the papal bull, which was promptly done. At the same time the nobles, their land sitting and the crops wasting in the fields, turned to their most familiar tool in an effort to force the mass of crusader serfs back to their peonage. They used intimidation, threatening the serfs and their families. They used force on anyone trying to join the crusade, and a number of families were slaughtered as examples. On May 23, just over a month later, the crusade was officially suspended.

Dozsa, the Transylvanian noble and sympathizer to the serf's plight, called a meeting of the "crusades" leaders. Rather than see the serfs go back to the same intolerable conditions they had fled, he drew up a program that called for an end to all the privileges of the nobility. Dozsa also called for the dividing of land among the poor, equality for everyone on the same level under church law (I'll bet you thought those were new revolutionary ideas) and a full-scale revolution. The core would be the army already gathered, but he called for every serf to rise up in support. They did. Fields were burned, masters slaughtered, monasteries and homes burned. It was most certainly a rural preview of the worst of the French Revolution that would occur two hundred and fifty years later.

For weeks Hungary descended into anarchy and chaos. Then another Transylvanian, Janos Zapolya, was hired and the well-trained regular military forces he led rather easily crushed the still disorganized and poorly armed crusader serfs. Within a few months they had once again enforced order on the countryside. Anyone thought to have led or abetted the serfs was executed, and the serfs were legally bound even more tightly to the land. Gyorgy Dozsa was brutally executed and his closest followers forced to eat his charred flesh.

By October the crusade and its aftermath were a bitter memory. Those serfs who remained alive harvested the crops, famine was averted, and for a few years things seemed to return to normal. At least 70,000 nobles and serfs died in those six bitter months. Entire families were wiped out and the entire economy of Hungary was seriously weakened. The Turks, peace treaty and all, were soon poised to take advantage of their neighbor's new weakness. Worse yet, the idea of such a revolt was firmly planted in the minds of everyone in Europe. Ten years later the peasants' revolt in Germany lasted almost a year. Much later the revolts in 1776 America and in 1789 France permanently changed Europe and the world.

Thousands died, the country was impoverished and a good percentage of the nobility slaughtered. What could you expect when you arm 100,000 oppressed and resentful serfs? No crusade ever got started, and a good percentage of the nobility was dead all because of one lapse of judgment. Clerics were protected and privileged. Was the cardinal a bit out of touch? Not much debate there. You do have to wonder how he felt at the end of the revolt.

You Chose Whom to Be the What?

Including this set of high-profile mistakes was a no-brainer. The problem with being a king, and an important one at that, was that your mistakes tended to have rather major consequences. Such as when the desire for a male heir, a necessary thing for a stable succession, changed the face of both politics and religion in the sixteenth century.

THE PROBLEMATIC PERSONNEL DECISIONS OF HENRY VIII
ENGLAND, 1535

Brian M. Thomsen

The term "Renaissance man" is perfectly applied to King Henry VIII, who ruled England from 1509 to 1547. In addition to matters of state, Henry was an accomplished lute player, composer, and poet, with a passion for drama, wrestling, hunting, and, of course, women. His wife problems (all six of them) are now the stuff of legend, though it must be duly noted that two of his nuptials were not really his fault.

The first, Catherine of Aragon, he quite literally inherited from his sickly unto death brother, and to say that she was not of his choosing would be an understatement. So when she had passed her childbearing years (as she was more than a bit older than Henry) and had born only a daughter, Henry quickly opted to have her replaced for the "good of succession" and undoubtedly his sex life.

Likewise the fourth marriage, to Anne of Cleves, was primarily a matter of state that evolved beyond his own control. After having shown Henry a portrait of her, Henry's chief advisor, Thomas Cromwell, had arranged the nuptial as a means of allying England closer diplomatically with Germany. The portrait turned out to be neither recent nor accurate, and as a result Henry quickly set in motion maneuvers to disengage himself from a wife he considered to be both old and ugly.

As a result, neither failed marriage can be considered Henry's fault or the product of poor choices on his part. The other four, however, resulted in two executions (Anne Boleyn and Katherine Howard), one death in childbed (Jane Seymour), and one who outlived him (Catherine Parr), whom he might also have divorced had he lived long enough.

One might be tempted to say that though Henry was intelligent, he was also less than skilled in matters of personal choice and choice of personnel, and nowhere was this better illustrated than in his choice of Sir Thomas More as chancellor during one of England's most turbulent times.

Thomas More (1478–1535) was a more contemplative Renaissance man than the king and no less intellectually talented. The son of a judge, he served as a page in the household of the archbishop and later went on to study at Oxford, where he excelled in the classics before moving on to the study of law, and after a short sojourn when he contemplated embracing religious monastic life, he became a barrister in 1501 and entered Parliament in 1505.

While practicing law became his day job, More still maintained contact with his scholarly side, conversing and debating with intellectual frater Desiderius Erasmus (author of the classic philosophical work *In Praise of Folly,* which is dedicated to More), even taking time to author various discourses and cerebral tracts such as *Utopia.* In addition to his scholastic profile, More also maintained a bit of the monastic side of his personality, reveling in a quasi-ascetic lifestyle despite the expansion of his and his family's fortunes over the years.

As a politician More was fearless in his arguments with the Crown. One of his first acts in Parliament was to urge a decrease in the appropriations for Henry VII (Henry VIII's predecessor). He did this with such vigor and vehemence that the king had More's father imprisoned until a hefty fine was paid.

After Henry VIII achieved the throne, More was appointed undersheriff of London, where he quickly achieved a profile as a careful and fair jurist. He also served as an arbiter for disputes about the wool trade and was instrumental in quelling an uprising in London. The scholar-barrister proved truly adept at arguing out pragmatic solutions to difficult situations and, as a result, quickly caught the eye of the young king, who appointed him to his royal privy council in 1518 and knighted him in 1521.

In a court populated with pandering oafs and bombastic brutes, Henry enjoyed the scholar's keen mind and engaged him in intellectual debate on a variety of subjects, even collaborating with him on his repudiation of the teachings of Martin Luther entitled "Defense of the Seven Sacraments." Their debates became quite spirited and Henry elevated More to Speaker of the House of Commons in 1523 (during which tenure More initiated the concept of parliamentary free speech) and chancellor of the duchy of Lancaster in 1525.

More had become the equivalent of Henry's oratorical

wrestling partner, engaging the king in debate on matters of law, diplomacy, philosophy and theology, much to the sovereign's intellectual delight. Unlike others in the royal circle, More had proven himself to be the king's mental equal, and as a result a subtle kinship was fostered between the precocious ruler and the ascetic lawyer. More than associates or royal and subject, the two actually became friends . . . at least for a time.

Others in his circle were continually disappointing the king. Even his lord chancellor Cardinal Wolsey had failed to reach an acceptable settlement with the pope concerning the king's desired divorce.

Henry knew he needed someone he could trust.

Henry knew he needed someone who could argue on his behalf.

Henry needed a friend and he needed a lawyer, and in Thomas More he saw the solution to all of his problems.

So in 1529, Wolsey was out and More was in, despite the fact that it was totally unconventional to appoint a layperson to that particular office. More's lay status might even be a plus in some of the negotiations that lay ahead, or at least so the king thought.

Henry's problem with the pope was simple: the state had arranged a dispensation for him to marry his brother's widow, and now he needed an annulment so that he could marry Anne Boleyn in hopes of securing a male heir to the throne. The problem was that Rome saw this as problematic, as from a canon law position it was tantamount to them saying they were wrong to have granted the first dispensation. As a result, given Wolsey's failure to win the church over to Henry's way of thinking, church and state were at loggerheads, and neither side would budge.

As detailed in "One Dispensation Too Many" (from *It Seemed*

Like a Good Idea, the prequel to this volume), Henry came up with an outside-of-the-box solution to the pesky inconvenience of being excommunicated—namely, forming the Church of England.

One can easily see where Henry's choice of More as Wolsey's successor might have seemed like an ideal solution, since More's lay affiliation easily circumvented such spiritual matters as vows of obedience and sovereignty of the pope as required of members of the clergy.

Unfortunately, Henry misjudged More.

Not only did Sir Thomas oppose in principle the king's "blas-phemous" deed (probably due to More's still strong monastic streak, which was probably more of a dominant part of his life than that of his predecessors in the position, despite their clerical affiliations), but he considered it equally bad to appear as if he condoned the action in any way, going so far as failing to attend the king's coronation of Anne as his queen.

Moreover, the sharp legal mind that the king had assumed was going to be used on his behalf was instead preoccupied with the parsing of the matter at hand in such a way as to benefit/protect the chancellor himself rather than to support the king's desired position. As a result, More soon fell out of favor, and he resigned his office in hopes of avoiding the need to personally confront this issue any longer.

Henry could not tolerate such lawyerly disloyalty and enacted "the Act of Succession" and "the Oath of Supremacy," which legally codified his position, securing it and preventing any lawyer from ever saying he was less than the rightful king.

More, though he did not publicly refute or denounce the act and oath, refused to swear and affirm it by using lawyerly weasel language that yet again neither lent support to the king's position nor incriminated himself as a traitor.

Eventually, though, even lawyers run out of tricks, and Thomas More was convicted of treason in a very ugly trial and executed, all because he refused to affirm the king's position over Rome.

Unlike Wolsey, who had tried to argue a means to the desired end in the tradition of most amoral lawyers, More refused to subvert his craft in the aiding and abetting of the subversion of the beliefs that he held dear.

When Henry appointed More high chancellor, the king assumed that he had appointed a conscientious lawyer; unfortunately, what he wound up with was a lawyer with a conscience.

More was, of course, not the only trusted advisor that Henry sent off to the executioner. Cardinal Wolsey, whom More had succeeded, was removed from office for failing to be effectual in dealing with the pope and arrested, and probably would have been executed had he not died before his trial. Thomas Cromwell, one of More's successors, was also executed for a truly unpardonable offense—the aforementioned betrothal of the king to the homely and old Anne of Cleves.

You Bought What?

Now here is a tale of real flower power. Sort of . . .

TULIPOMANIA
NETHERLANDS, 1636

Paul Kupperberg

Capitalism isn't the road to riches for everyone. Take the examples of the 1990s dot-com boom and bust, or the 1929 stockmarket crash (as well as a series of disastrous depressions across earlier decades), not to mention the imploding speculative European market disaster known as the South Sea Bubble of the early eighteenth century.

And the curious case in the United Provinces of the Netherlands of 1636 that came to be known as Tulipomania.

The mania for the buying and selling of tulips might sound as though it were more in league with the trading of collectibles like baseball cards, comic books, or Beanie Babies, but this floral fever exploded into a full-blown economic frenzy that touched every strata of Dutch society. In the course of about a year, prices of tulip bulbs sold among the usually sensible population of Holland went from reasonable to outlandish. A single rare bulb could be—and was!—traded for an entire estate, landholdings and all. Tradesmen sold their businesses and plowed the profits into the tulip trade. It was the first futures market in the world. Fortunes were made in a single transaction, while even greater riches were lost in the headlong rush of speculators fleeing the collapsing market. The legal entanglements that ensued were so complex, legislators finally threw up their hands in surrender and left it for local courts to figure out.

All this over the simple, elegant tulip—and man's seeming inability to avoid being sucked into even the most ludicrous fits of speculation when the smell of a fast buck was in the air.

While the names of some of the culprits of this floral bubble have been lost to history, their deeds live on, as in the case of a house in the town of Hoorn with three stone tulips carved into its façade, commemorating its sale in 1633 for the price of three rare tulips. It's here that many believe the Dutch mania for tulips began, when word spread that someone had sold his entire house *for three flowers!*

Known among botanists by the name *Tulipa* (derived from the Turkish word *tulpend,* or "turban," which the flower resembles), the wild variety of the flower is native to Turkey and western and central Asia. Though a few species occur in Europe, and though we've come to think of Holland as the home of the tulip, the flower was unknown there until sometime in the sixteenth century. Tulips had been cultivated in Turkey for centuries before they found their way into the gardens—and economic history—of the Netherlands, thanks to the botanist Carolus Clusius. The aged scientist brought the flower home with him from a visit to Constantinople in 1593 to the University of Leiden for purposes of medicinal research. Though always happy to share his finds with fellow scientists—Clusius was a respected researcher and writer on medicine and pharmacy in addition to botany—he refused to sell any of his rare tulips to envious neighbors who sought this new plant for their gardens. Of course, to be fair—and to help explain the scarcity in the coming craze—tulips can be grown from either seed (a slow—some six or seven years—and chancy process for achieving a specific variety of flower) or by producing offsets, or outgrowths, of the mother bulb, which become flowering bulbs in their own right within a year or two. A bulb, however, can produce only two or three offsets a year for only a couple of years before the mother bulb is depleted.

At least one of Clusius's neighbors figured a way around the old scientist's reluctance to part with his precious plants. He stole the bulbs right out of his garden.

Soon thereafter, tulips began sprouting in the gardens of many of the Dutch merchant class, men newly made rich by the lucrative East Indies trade and not shy about displaying their wealth. The number of the cultivated varieties of these lovely blooms increased quickly in the hands of their Dutch growers, producing thirteen new groups of tulips with names like Couleren, Bizarden, Violetten, Marquertrinen, and Rosen, each of which could have produced literally hundreds of varieties, all based on their color schemes. The flowers were explosions of brilliant hues, solid and striped, some with gilded edges, some veined with startling flames and flares of contrasting colors. Purples and reds and yellows and pinks, purples and browns, colors more intense than anything else in the gardens of Holland. The tulip soon became the rage; indeed, possessing a collection of these lovely blooms was seen as evidence of taste and breeding among the rich. Wanting to also be viewed as tasteful and well bred, the middle class soon joined in the mania and, throughout the early part of the century, the price of tulip bulbs rose at a steady pace.

The first superstar of the tulip world was the celebrated Semper Augustus, a flower of the Rosen group of such breathtakingly intense reds and vivid blues and whites that it was universally hailed as the finest tulip ever grown. Again, its owner's name was lost—or withheld—by history, but by 1624, all the estimated one dozen examples of this rare flower were in the hands of this single man. Offers were made to buy bulbs of this rare bit of beauty, but the man spurned them all in favor of keeping the majestic bloom to himself. It was reported that offers as high as two to three thousand guilders (one guilder was the approximate daily wage for a Dutch craftsman) were put on the table for a single Semper Augustus bulb. The inability to lay their hands on this most precious of the precious flowers drove the rest of the Dutch connoisseurs mad with envy, and they tried to retaliate by pushing the best specimens of their own collections to rival in both beauty and value the Semper Augustus. None ever succeeded. But this desire to own what they couldn't have caused competition between collectors to grow and, more important, prices to push upward at a faster pace than before.

In his 1841 study of the crowd mentality, *Extraordinary Popular Delusions and the Madness of Crowds*, Charles Mackay wrote, "In reading the history of nations, we find that, like individuals, they have their whims and their peculiarities; their seasons of excitement and recklessness, when they care not what they do. We find that whole communities suddenly fix their minds upon one object, and go mad in its pursuit; that millions of people become simultaneously impressed with one delusion, and run after it, till their attention was caught by some new folly more captivating than the first." While Mackay was writing about the behavior of people in general, that description perfectly fits the Dutch of 1636–1637. The craze to own tulips and, more important, to sell them for huge sums of money or goods suddenly jumped from the upper classes to spread like head lice through every level of Dutch society. It became an all-consuming mania. Anyone with a few stuivers to rub together was jumping on the tulip bandwagon, with an informal network of futures markets setting up in hundreds of taverns across Holland.

By the winter of 1636–1637, the Netherlands was at the height of the tulip frenzy. Bulbs could be bought and sold a dozen times in a day—all while lying dormant in someone's home or garden. Since tulips bloom only for a few days a year, these people weren't even buying pretty, vibrant flowers; they were laying their life savings on a bulb that strongly resembled an onion (indeed, there's the likely apocryphal story of a sailor mistakenly slicing up and consuming a valuable Semper Augustus bulb with his herring in the home of a wealthy merchant). Weavers sold their looms, farmers their lands and equipment, blacksmiths their forges to get their hands on the money to dive into bulb trading. A group of professional tulip traders, called florists, soon evolved, and money was being made everywhere by nearly everyone, much of it on paper in the form of futures—an agreed-upon price of a specific bulb at a specific time in the future. The tulip trade, because it dealt in a product that its buyers seldom saw, came to be known as the Wind Trade. But the harder the wind blew, the higher the prices rose, and not even the sky seemed the limit.

Then came the February 5, 1637, auction of the estate of Wouter Bartelmiesz Winkel, one of the richest men in the town of Alkmaar. Wouter Winkel had managed to acquire through shrewd trading a valuable collection of some seventy-five top-of-the-line specimens—in addition to a goodly load of more common, though still valuable, flowers—including a rare Admirael van Enkhuizen, some Viceroys and various Brabansons, not to mention a few rare Rosen Admirael van de Eijacks, and others. After his death, his seven orphaned children were left to collect the proceeds of the auction: almost 90,000 guilders!

Though on the face of it the Wouter Winkel auction appears to have been a good thing for the Wind Trade, it seemed instead to have been the straw that broke the camel's back. Indeed, just two days earlier, in a tavern in the city of Haarlem, in a regular trading session of florists, an offering of tulips did not sell, even after the auctioneer repeatedly dropped the price. Word spread across Haarlem, then to other trading towns, and with it went a panic that grew at an even faster pace than the mania that preceded it. It was as though those few fateful minutes in that Haarlem tavern were the reawakening of common sense among the speculators, a feeling that, like the contents of Pandora's box, once unleashed could not be recalled.

Prices plummeted. A tulip worth 5,000 guilders before February 3 sold for 50 guilders soon thereafter. The fortunate speculator would see a 5 percent return on his prebust investment; most would be lucky to get back 1 percent of what they invested.

Of course, Tulipomania was a bubble built on a dream, a case of supply and demand tripping over one another for a few frantic months until finally neither could stand. And, as was her wont, Mother Nature had the last laugh on the speculators and opportunists: in the wild, tulips were a solid color, usually red, yellow, or white, unlike their cultivated brethren. The cause of the riot and intensity of colors and varieties of Dutch tulips, including the most highly valued Semper Augustus, was a virus, a disease unique to the tulip!

In the end, the Dutch mania for tulips cost many of the speculators, collectors, and florists fortunes that were never to be recovered. Unlike later speculative bubbles that burst after over-expansion, Tulipomania never did reach into the core of the nation's economy. Private fortunes and personal holdings were lost to the tune of uncounted millions of guilders—again, many of these fortunes existed only on paper to begin with—but the Amsterdam stock exchange kept well away from the Wind Trade. Thus, the effects on the Dutch economy were negligible at best, but it remains a national embarrassment and, of course, a handy object lesson with which the pundits can chide modern-day dot-commers ... even as they continue to stock up on scarce Beanie Babies and rare Pokémon and Magic cards as a hedge against the future. And a future opportunity to retell the rise and fall of Tulipomania.

You Sent Whom, Governor?

It seems no one is immune from the occasional colossal blunder. In this case the blunderer did rather better later on in life, at least to the thinking of most Americans. A few British may still harbor a different opinion.

GEORGE WASHINGTON
"NEVER SEND A BOY TO DO A MAN'S JOB"
AMERICA, 1753–1754

Paul A. Thomsen

Later he became the "father of his country," but in the beginning George Washington was less than a great leader. As a young man, George Washington longed for a life of adventure and exploration, but a manipulative mother, a collection of needy siblings, and the intricate affairs of his family's Virginia plantation conspired to keep him close to home.

In 1753, Washington indulged his growing hunger for adventure as a "weekend warrior" in Virginia's colonial militia. However, after months of dress and military study passed, the young Virginian still craved a life apart from home and hearth. Thus when his colonial governor, Robert Dinwiddie, offered Washington the chance to help settle a key colonial dispute far away in the French-controlled Ohio Valley, the young Virginian jumped at the opportunity.

European troubles were bound to visit the American continent, but for close to two hundred years cool heads and collected
colonial minds had managed to keep Europe's wars Europe's
affairs. While England and France argued for decades over the
proper demarcation lines between their two major American colonial holdings, each actually had little impetus to resolve the matters of minor backwater border disputes in the American Ohio
Valley. England's hands-off approach, however, worried their
Virginian colony as rumors began to fly over a regional French military buildup. When word eventually reached the colonial powers
that their centuries-old neighbors/adversaries were actually building fortifications on lands claimed by the distant Virginians, it
seemed imperative for the colonials to send a representative to the
French-claimed area with an eye for detail, a quiet demeanor, and
a steady hand with which one might convey to the French an ultimatum to depart the contested land. Though whoever went, the
French garrisons, trappers, and most natives were likely to see him
as he was, more of a spy than a messenger.

Though other Virginian men were more senior in rank and had
greater experience, they begged off the dangerous opportunity.
With nowhere else to turn, on October 31, 1753, Governor Robert
Dinwiddie offered the position to the energetic, albeit inexperienced, twenty-one-year-old George Washington. Holding the rank
of major and having served as a part-time surveyor, Washington
was expected to traverse the rugged and largely untraveled countryside, descend into the Ohio Valley, make notes on the French
force he encountered, deliver his colony's message, and return
promptly home with the naively expected French response of compliance. It was a daunting prospect for the young Virginian, but

remembering the ingenuity exhibited by his father and half brother
years prior (one as a frontier leader, and the other while serving a
tour of duty in the British military's Caribbean campaign), and
perhaps sensing some special insight in the boy, Dinwiddie was
convinced George Washington would do his family, his colony
and his empire well.

Major George Washington's party departed for the wilderness
before the first day was out. Struggling through heavy bouts of pre-
cipitation and early winter winds, the company soon reached the
forked Ohio River (present-day Pittsburgh). Christopher Gist, the
party's backwoodsman, led the group to a nearby locale favored by
Iroquois natives loyal to the English Crown, hoping to gain a native
guide to speed their journey. Major Washington held ulterior
motives for the stopover however. He wanted to convince the
region's tribal leader, the Half-King, to provide the Virginians with
an armed escort of tribal braves to the French lines. The young officer thought that if he conducted the pending meeting properly, the
party's arrival at the French fortification, augmented by numerous
regional natives, would convey a strong show of force and ensure
their shared adversaries compliance with the intended ultimatum.

Reality, however, intervened.

When the young and naive Major Washington was finally
awarded an audience with the Half-King, his plans came undone
by his inexperience through both breaches in tribal etiquette
(Washington speaking before he was recognized as having the
floor), and the Virginian's prejudiced perspective of tribal political
structure.

The Half-King was understanding of Washington's impetuousness and personally took no offense, but his tribe was not of a similar

mind. After the Half-King publicly acceded to Major Washington's wishes and the English emissary retired for the night, a loud and angry debate erupted among the tribal members over the impetuosity of this man. The next morning the Virginians awoke to find the complete services offered by the Half-King to be reduced to a hunter and three aged chiefs (including the disdainful Half-King), the remainder of the tribe having apparently refused to risk their lives for the willful Virginian's unspoken mission.

Though disheartened, George Washington accepted the Half-King and his men into the party and departed the camp as quickly as they could gather their belongings.

During the long native-guided journey toward the French lines, Washington listened to the Half-King tirelessly rage and threaten action against their shared neighbor. The tribal leader appeared to grow ever more bitter toward the French with each passing mile, and Washington became less and less sure of his small band of native scouts. Over time the Virginian began to see the ragtag band of natives as a sign of British impotence and as a potentially destabilizing element in confronting the French.

Their situation was a powder keg ready to blow.

The Virginian would have gladly thanked the Half-King and his men for their time and sent them back to their encampment, yet neither George Washington nor his group knew the surrounding area. Furthermore, burdened by other responsibilities, Washington had not so much as a clue as to how to return to the Half-King's camp, let alone return east. As the party neared the French encampment, Major Washington convinced the Iroquois to remain behind, encamped within the nearby woods, and hopefully out of sight.

When the unencumbered party reached the nearest French outpost (a small forward structure with only the barest complement of
French forces), Washington's men were dutifully conducted inside
and introduced to the French-Indian negotiator Philippe Thomas
de Joncaire, sieur de Chabert (a living legend who held great sway
over the region's Native Americans). Though unnerved by the
Seneca-raised Frenchman's presence, Major Washington was
silently thankful that his new traveling companions had remained
out of sight. As Major Washington explained the party's need to
convey an urgent message to his host's superiors, they were
informed that the person with whom they needed to speak was
actually sixty miles upriver; but given the rapid approach of night,
de Joncaire offered Major Washington and his men a good dinner
and their outpost's meager comforts before resuming their journey
at dawn. Washington's complement did not refuse the questionable invitation.

While his fellows drank deeply of French wine and gave themselves to inebriation, George Washington remained aloof, wincing
at the laxness of his men's mouths and dutifully noting every exaggerated French reply. Eventually, Washington was asked about a
nearby native encampment. Answering in truth, Major Washington
subsequently watched with dread as de Joncaire promptly invited
the Half-King and his men inside for a drink. Coming to terms with
the fear that his mission was rapidly approaching a hostile and possibly terminal conclusion, the Virginian braced for the Iroquois
leader's well-prepared speech. However, instead of hearing ire and
righteousness blast from the native leader's mouth upon his
entrance, Washington witnessed the Half-King's contingent enter,
embrace the French offerings of wine, and grow steadily drunk as

the night grew long. Rather than watch the continuing spectacle (and possibly redeem the evening with a sober witness to slipped French secrets), George Washington retired for the night in disgust.

The next morning the party set out once more. After trekking nearly five more days over snow- and rain-driven swamplands, Major Washington's party finally reached the log-encased French fortification of Le Boeuf. Presenting his colony's mandate to the French commandant, Legardeur de St. Pierre, George Washington was granted free reign of the French fortification, if he would only wait for a response. Concealing his surprise, Major Washington accepted the offer.

Walking freely about the walled camp, he eyed the fortification's strong wall, able complement of men, ample supplies and weaponry. As he noted the facts and figures for his pending report to Dinwiddie, George Washington felt a sinking feeling. The French, he thought, had allowed this self-guided tour as a gesture of military superiority and contempt for their English neighbors. Major Washington's suspicions reached self-validation when he returned to the French commander's office and read St. Pierre's refutation of the Virginian ultimatum, claiming he would convey the message to his superiors in France, but ". . . As to the summons you send me to retire, I do not think myself obliged to obey it." To the young Virginian's eyes, the French were preparing for war.

Propelled by his fears, Major Washington promptly departed the French fortification. His attempt to return to Virginia as quickly as possible was, however, hampered by the almost constant downpour, which had now turned entirely to snow. With streams freezing and travel via canoe now useless, the party turned to travel on horseback. The going slower than he would have liked, Major Washington gave himself once more to impetuousness and, dressing in a Native American matchcoat, broke ranks with his Virginian guide.

Proceeding on foot with the backwoodsman Christopher Gist as his sole companion, Major Washington risked his life and the little knowledge he had gained on the merciless Ohio Valley winter. Making better time than their now distant party, the two men soon came upon two natives. Hoping to obtain swift yet safe passage, Major Washington asked if they might see himself and Gist through into Virginia proper. The natives readily agreed, but a short time later, the two colonials suddenly found themselves being led into an open field.

According to later accounts, the lead native then pulled free his rifle, spun around, leveled it, and discharged his round at the two Virginians. Miraculously, the two travelers remained unharmed as the shot went wide. Christopher Gist grabbed the native and was about to reciprocate the man's intention when Major Washington ordered him to desist. Apparently against his better judgment (and the realization of possibly being hunted by others nearby), Gist turned the would-be assassin loose. The two shaken colonials then fled the scene with deliberate speed.

Arriving in Williamsburg on January 16, 1754, George Washington offered his report as well as his diary detailing the journey's daily events via messenger to Governor Robert Dinwiddie. Washington realized that the more powerful the French appeared, the less embarrassing his failure to send them off would be. Greatly alarmed by the somewhat exaggerated picture George Washington had painted, Dinwiddie shared the discovery with others and ordered Washington to publish his diary as evidence of the perceived impending French aggression.

Returning home, George Washington was lauded as a hero. He reported to Governor Dinwiddie of his hazardous journey, his contact with the Half-King, his meeting with the French and their seemingly resilient Ohio Valley force of occupation. Washington also told of his belief that the French were certainly preparing to advance their American holdings by force, if necessary. With Washington's thoughts and deeds, Governor Dinwiddie rallied the General Assembly. The French, he charged, could be marching into Virginia` proper and there would be little they could do to hold the British line. In response, the Virginian government hastily organized a military force and sent them to erect their own forward post in the wilderness.

Events steadily spiraled out of control. France, of course, quickly reacted to the Virginian fortification (perceived as an attempt at land-grabbing), and destroyed the structure before it could be completed. George Washington, hero and Ohio Valley expert, was ordered back into the contested area at the head of a new mixed complement of armed men and loyal natives. Charged with foiling the French seizure, Washington was party to Britain's first defeat in the French and Indian War. He returned home in disgrace and disgust, wanting nothing further to do with exploration or adventure.

Though Washington grew into the character and role of the victorious general of an ill-trained and poorly equipped army of colonials during the American Revolution, Dinwiddie had failed to see the untested, untempered boy inside young George Washington. While Washington would later emerge as a military strategist, tactician, and warrior like few others, he had been unable to properly divine a way through his troubled odyssey through the Ohio Valley. Washington had also failed to realize that

France's American fortifications were actually modest defensive structures far removed from Virginian lines, that the human intelligence he had gathered had largely come from questionable sources and suppositions, that the native populace of the Ohio Valley actually cared little for either side, and that France realistically had little time or money to take the prized remote and undeveloped region.

In actuality, young George Washington's inexperience and untrained eye actually upset the entire Western Hemisphere's geopolitical landscape. He single-handedly brought about the French and British war for America. This led to the need to permanently station British regiments in the American colonies and, as a result, the tea and stamp taxes to support them. The housing of these regular army units imposed on ordinary citizens and the taxation were the proximate causes for the first colonial movements, which were established only to try to gain for colonials "the rights of all British Citizens and eventually blossomed into the War for Independence, the American Revolution.

In a way things did work out in the long run. The explosive report of an inexperienced youth and the disastrous military expedition it inspired did much to precipitate the events of both the American War for Independence and the French Revolution. But you have to feel how the ambitious and proud young George Washington felt as his disaster became the talk of Virginia. Later he was the hero of a Revolution. Strangely it was a revolution that might never have happened except for the consequences of his own youthful mistakes.

You Lost Your Head

It was the worst of times, yep, the worst of times, and not the best of times at all. That certainly turned out to be the case for the man who made the decisions at the height of the French Revolution. His decisions definitely ensured the worst of endings for him.

ROBESPIERRE'S ELOQUENCE AND FATALLY BAD TIMING
IN BEING WOUNDED
PARIS, 1794

Brian M. Thomsen

The French Revolution was actually a series of revolutions that redefined the governing powers of the French empires in a gradual and violent shift that eventually replaced an absolutely powerful sovereign (as best exemplified by Louis XIV, who was, after a long reign of total monarchical control, long dead before the power shifts began to occur) with a series of temporary governmental bodies, which shifted further and further to the left politically and often based their powers on the blunt force of mob rule.

What actually caused the Revolution(s) is still subject to debate. The common populist myth of French peasants starving after years of famine and oppression, with a tyrannical military force unjustly imprisoning thousands, is at best an exaggeration. The iconographic image of the peasants storming the Bastille, though inspiring, is actually of little consequence pragmatically since the prison itself, at the time, was really incarcerating only a few madmen and a handful of common criminals who were neither political nor of the type that the stormers would really have wanted to free.

True, the country was in debt from foreign wars and extravagant expenditures on the elegant lifestyle of the ruling family, but such matters really did not concern the peasant class, whose hard-lot lives were relatively consistent from year to year. The group that was really affected was the aristocracy, who were still licking their wounds from years of gelding impotence at the hands of Louis XIV, who kept his nobles powerless and preoccupied. Now the nobles saw the present weaker monarchy of Louis XVI, who was neither as bright nor as politically savvy as his predecessors, as an opportunity to make a power grab.

Unfortunately their years of gilded confinement in Versailles had made them less savvy and capable of governing, which opened the door to authority to a new class of educated non-nobles who had embraced the philosophic theories of the Enlightenment that called for a new social order. The most dangerous members of this newly empowered bourgeoisie were the lawyers, and in particular one by the name of Robespierre.

Maximilien-François-Marie-Isadore de Robespierre was born, the product of the seduction of a brewer's daughter by a smooth-talking lawyer, at Arras in 1758. His parents reluctantly wed and continued on a downward spiral that produced three more children, who along with Maximilien were eventually raised by relatives after their mother died in childbirth, while their father never recovered from the grief of her loss.

The relatives secured young Robespierre a good education and he eventually advanced to the College of Law in Paris, which enabled him to return to Arras and establish his own legal practice in a much more successful manner than his father had ever achieved.

His eloquence both verbally and scripturally was all too apparent through his involvement in numerous philosophic circles and literary societies. This so impressed his local constituency that he was eventually elected to the position of deputy of Artois to the Estates General on the eve of the French Revolution. He quickly advanced through the other bourgeoisie power brokers to the National Constituent Assembly, where his oratorical skills fully blossomed in the public eye, distinguishing him from much of the political rabble that was jockeying for position and advancement within the anarchical situation that was getting more and more dangerous by the moment.

Robespierre's own political views had been greatly influenced by the works of Jean-Jacques Rousseau, whose maxims and theories on equality and community he quickly appropriated, impressing many of his lesser-well-read contemporaries.

Robespierre's greatest weapon was his tongue, which he wielded with eloquent and deadly precision. When the National Constituent Assembly was dissolved in 1791, he had amassed a devoted following, not just among his "equals" but among the street-level rabble as well, who regarded him as an "incorruptible patriot," a designation thought by many to be quite paradoxical given his societal position as both an attorney and a politician. At the show trial for King Louis XVI that followed the mobs taking over Paris in the name of the people, Robespierre put forth the argument that Louis's fate was not to be charged in reference to that of a single man but as a matter of public safety for all of the people of France:

"Louis must die that the country may live."

Even if the rabble didn't understand the lawyerly and philosophical underpinnings of his argument, they did understand what he was advising and the former king was sent to the guillotine on January 21, 1793.

As the Revolution moved to the left, many aristocrats were forced into exile or prison, and many bourgeoisie politicos who had served in the government under the king and during the interim were forced to seek safer circumstances outside of France in order to avoid fates similar to those they originally condemned. After that Robespierre managed to continue to ride the revolutionary wave propelled by his gilded tongue and persuasive arguments, attaining a position on the now-ruling Committee of Public Safety while also marinating ties and allegiances with those of the further left, who still managed to incite the mob and feed the revolutionary fervor.

Buttressed by fears of invasion from abroad as well as widespread corruption within France, Robespierre and his followers established the so-called Reign of Terror, during which they systematically set about purifying France of its enemies and those who weakened the public safety (this included anyone who did not embrace the Rousseauian philosophies as eloquently espoused by their oratorical leader). In no time at all former friends and associates found themselves marching to Madame Guillotine due to disagreements with the party will.

Robespierre ascended to the presidency of the Convention on June 4, 1794, and quickly engineered reforms to accelerate the sys-

tem of justice he had put in place. Courts were replaced by tri-
bunals, and the calling of witnesses on behalf of the accused was
virtually eliminated. In roughly a month, about a thousand people
were executed for various political crimes against the state, with
nary a voice spoken in opposition to the silken tones of the bloodstained president.

The other members of the ruling convention began to fear the
hold that this man had on the crowd and, further encouraged by
French military victories abroad, which seemed to have eliminated
the fear of invasion by the monarchies that controlled the rest of
Europe, moved to have him overthrown.

By the end of July, Robespierre and some of his followers were
arrested and held incommunicado while charged with tyranny
under the same code of silence that had functioned during his
Reign of Terror.

Robespierre was not worried. Barred from speaking in his own
defense to the Convention, he would address his own power
base—the mob in the streets.

Quickly he and the other prisoners engineered an escape with
the help of soldiers loyal to the Commune of Paris rather than the
Convention itself, and the group quickly retreated to the Hotel de
Ville, where Robespierre made ready the speech with which he
would once again woo the crowd to his will.

The officers of the Convention dispatched the National Guard
to recapture this most dangerous of agitators and most gifted of
orators as soon as possible. Robespierre was injured during the
scuffle, though there is some debate over whether the gunshot that
hit him was fired by accident by one of his supporters, by himself,
or by the National Guardsmen.

The delay of preparation for his speech and the duress of their defense during the recapture had deprived the orator from having his say to the crowd, and the wound he sustained made any attempt to talk his way back into the favor of those really in control, the mob and military, impossible because the pistol round had shattered his jaw. The next day the gilded tongue was silenced forever as Robespierre and twenty-one of his followers made their acquaintance with Madame Guillotine without a single word spoken in their defense.

You Are Shocking

There are many stories of great minds believing pure hogwash. Physicists of great stature have believed in séances. It just goes to show that even the sharpest mind can have a few blunt edges.

DR. ELISHA PERKINS AND GALVANISM

EUROPE, 1796

Jody Lynn Nye

Most people of today are familiar with the scene made famous in the 1931 movie *Frankenstein*: a monster, assembled from the parts of corpses, animated by the application of lightning. Mary Shelley, the author of the 1818 novel and widely held to be the mother of science fiction, knew of experiments going on throughout Europe that made use of the discoveries of Luigi Galvani. As do modern science fiction writers, she took the basic concept and extrapolated upon it to suggest that with the aid of another scientist's invention, Alessandro Volta's "Voltaic pile," or, as we know it today, the battery, one could revive dead tissue not only to move but to think. To the horror of many contemporary readers, Mary Shelley allowed her protagonist, Dr. Victor Frankenstein, to create life, thrusting him into the role of God.

The scientists themselves may have had similar delusions of grandeur. The use of electricity as an experimental and medical tool is reported to have begun as an observation at the dinner table. Galvani's wife, Lucia, had prepared frogs' legs for dinner. Luigi noticed that one of them was still twitching. He believed that the effect was caused by a latent power he called animal electricity conducted to the muscles by a fluid. He devised an electrostatic machine so that he could duplicate the effect he witnessed.

His investigations were followed very soon by many other thinkers, but it was not until 1800, when Volta's electrical storage system made sensational public displays of the theory possible, that the general public joined the debate. Giovanni Aldini, Galvani's nephew, performed public demonstrations in London in 1802 during which he applied current to nerves in the bodies of executed criminals, causing facial contortions and spontaneous muscular contractions.

As with all new inventions, the promoters suggested that electrical current could revolutionize medical science. Dr. Andrew Ure, another scientist who offered a public show using a Voltaic pile, even suggested that it could restore life, a notion that probably influenced Mary Shelley. Over time, electricity and galvanism came to be associated with legitimate medical treatments such as electroshock therapy, muscle stimulation and acupuncture, but in the meanwhile, there was plenty of room for wrong thinking, scientific dead ends and downright fraud.

In the early part of the nineteenth century, philosophers were beginning to question standard medical practice. At the same time as Galvanism was gaining a following, so was Mesmerism and homeopathy. The public was eager to try new cures, which they hoped would be more effective than the ones in use at the time.

Into this period of open minds strode Dr. Elisha Perkins. In 1796, Perkins was expelled from the Connecticut Medical Society for quackery. He had invented a cure-all device for pain and gout that he called Tractors. Tractors were a pair of metal rods three inches long, pointed at one end and rounded at the other, one rod made of brass and the other of iron. They could be used by anyone, not requiring an attached battery to work their miracle. The practitioner, following the very complicated treatise that accompanied the device, stroked the affected part. Within a short time, if the treatment was performed correctly, the Tractors unblocked the "solar fluid" or "electrical matter" so it flowed unchecked through the body.

"Perkinism" became a fad. Perkins claimed that his device would cure "pains in the head, face, teeth, breast, side, stomach, back, rheumatism and some gouts." Reports of successes poured in. Even George Washington fell for the sales pitch and bought a pair. Apparently he found some relief with them, because Perkins obtained a letter of introduction from him to John Marshall of the Continental Congress. In 1799 Perkins tried to treat his own yellow fever with his Tractors, and died.

Benjamin Perkins, his son, renewed the patent on his father's invention and began to sell his devices in Europe. Jumping on the interest evoked by Galvani's experiments and Aldini's demonstrations, his advertisements suggested the Tractors worked because of the Galvanic principles. Sales increased, and more patients proclaimed that they had been cured, though those cures almost certainly owe their success to faith in the device and the placebo effect, not the Tractors.

Benjamin had all the instincts of a modern marketing genius.

To promote the device, he created the Perkinsean Institution in 1803 and commissioned a poem to be read at the opening, which went in part:

> See *Pointed Metals*, blest with power t'appease,
> The ruthless rage of merciless disease.
> O'er the frail part a subtil fluid pour,
> Drench'd with invisible Galvanic shower . . .

But whatever his glorious claims, the Tractors never produced more than temporary palliation of localized pain. Johan Daniel Herholdt, surgeon of the Royal Academy of Sciences in Copenhagen, conducted experiments using a pair of Tractors brought to him by the wife of an American army major. His results were only slightly satisfactory. He had not been given the fulsome accompanying treatise, so there was no added placebo effect. The Tractors went to Germany, where the Royal Physician tried them and added a few deprecatory notes of his own to those of the Danish scientists. Fortunately for Benjamin Perkins, he obtained the comments before they became available to the general public, rewrote the testimonials to favor Tractors, reasserting that they worked, as so many happy patients in the United States and Great Britain could attest.

Dr. John Haygarth, a debunker of Tractors, stated in his 1799 essay "*Of the Imagination, as a Cause and as a Cure of Disorders of the Body; Exemplified by Ficticious Tractors, and epidemical convulsions*," "An enthusiastick dupe of this doctrine can perform cures with incomparably greater success than the most skilful physician or surgeon, with the aid of the most pompous figures of geometry which can be described, or fictitious stories which can be related. Genuine enthusiasm is wonderfully infectious." Benjamin Perkins died in 1810 a wealthy man, his fortune made by harnessing the "electricity" of excitement and hope. Without him to boost them in the public eye, the Tractors disappeared almost completely by 1811. Sheepish customers probably threw them away, realizing that they had paid for an idea, not a cure.

You Married Whom?

Sometimes what should have been a great romance turns instead into a fatal attraction. This is even worse if the participants are royalty and the victim their countries.

FREDERICK OF PRUSSIA AND PRINCESS VICTORIA
GERMANY, 1858

Elizabeth Moon

Fritz and Vicky met first at the Great Exhibition. He was twenty; she was ten. They met again in Scotland, where he proposed to the vivacious girl, though she was then too young to marry. When Fritz married Vicky three years later, on January 25, 1858, her parents were delighted: this was the marriage they'd hoped and planned for. His relatives were less happy; they particularly resented her mother's insistence that she be married in her own church, at home, and they hoped Vicky would not be as strong-minded. The couple themselves were genuinely in love, both with each other and with ideas—they were intelligent, diligent, capable, and well intentioned.

They were also at the eye of a political hurricane: late-nineteenth-century Europe. Vicky—Victoria Adelaide Mary Louise—was Queen Victoria's oldest child; Fritz—Frederick, son of William (then regent for his mentally ill brother, but soon to be King of Prussia in his own right) was crown prince of Prussia and would become crown prince of a Germany united by Bismarck in 1871, a Germany which would be victorious in several wars (against Austria, Denmark, and finally France). Already, Prussia resented England's imperial might, its wealth and prestige. Prussia did not want a bossy English princess giving advice. But Prince Albert had influenced both Vicky and Frederick, and Vicky, like her mother, believed she had a mission to carry out her father's hopes for a peaceful, productive European society with constitutional governments.

While it may be hard to think of Queen Victoria and her children as liberals today, a glance into Prussian concepts of government will make it clear why they were so labeled.

The Prussians felt about Vicky the way Republicans feel about Hillary Clinton—she was a horrid, nasty, evil woman with *ideas*, albeit being only seventeen when she married—and they hated and distrusted her even before the marriage. Her parents, especially her father, had seen to her education; she was multilingual, extremely well read, and enthusiastic about the changes that Frederick might be able to make. She talked politics. She tried to—and actually did—influence her husband. Germans desired no such talents in women—women were to breed and, if noble, to dress well—and their hostility brought out reactive hostility from her.

She was, after all, the daughter of the greatest ruler of the greatest empire then existing. Growing up Victoria's eldest child did not—could not—make for sweet humility. She made no friends; she thought, and said that English ways were better than Prussian ways, in everything from food to footwear.

When her first child, William, was born, those who could not put a wedge between Vicky and Fritz began to insert one between this heir to the throne and his parents. Willy, as the family called him, was encouraged to blame everything he didn't like on his mother and on her nationality. (His brachial birth injury, resulting in a withered arm, was not her fault—he's the one who wiggled around into breech position and had to be pulled out.) The riding lessons he feared were her fault (though all riding in Germany, then and for long after, was taught using harsh methods and long, painful hours in the saddle). The long days of lessons were her fault; the sternness of his tutors was her fault (though Prussian methods of child rearing were a long way from Spock or Montessori). Prussia had long envied England's imperial might and reputation; Prussian dislike of England seeped into Willy through nurses, tutors, his grandfather, the men of the court.

When he was sent away to school, and then joined the Guards, he was surrounded by men who hated England and anything remotely liberal, and his dislike of his mother grew ever stronger. He got along well with his grandfather and with Bismarck; they formed a triumvirate that excluded Frederick and Vicky. The finale to his anger with his mother came with his father's fatal illness. Frederick contracted cancer of the throat. Early in the course of the illness, German doctors recommended radical surgery, removal of the larynx, which would have left Frederick mute (a serious disability for the future German emperor). Naturally the family were reluctant to take this step if it was not absolutely necessary. Both Willy and his grandfather forbade the surgery until another consultation had been made.

That consultation was with the presumably preeminent throat specialist of the era . . . who happened to be British. He insisted that the growth on Frederick's vocal cords was not from cancer but overuse, and prescribed months of rest in less stringent air than that of north Germany. Vicky and Fritz went to England.

But the growth was cancer and quickly grew past the point where surgery might save Frederick's life. Frederick's father had lived much longer than expected (he died at ninety-one), so Frederick had only ninety-nine days as kaiser before he died of cancer and Willy—known to history as Kaiser Wilhelm of World War I—took over.

Willy and much of the rest of Germany blamed Vicky for the misdiagnosis, for the trip to England, for her attempt to spare her husband worry and stress during the last months of his life. He set himself steadfastly against her and everything he believed she wanted or stood for.

None of the hopes and ambitions of Frederick and Vicky came to pass; the friendship between England and Germany that they both longed for—which Albert, Queen Victoria's husband, had longed for—was never to be. A stable, peaceful Europe, governed by enlightened constitutional monarchies, with ample resources for science and technology, with happy, productive citizens, would never exist.

Instead, Kaiser Wilhelm plunged eagerly, full of envy and pride, into the great arms race that produced great iron battleships, bigger guns, more poison gas, and detailed plans for invading neighboring countries, and into colonial expansion, expressing the racism and arrogance that were characteristic of not only his but, later, German ambition. Germany should be the one great world power, toppling Britain, overpowering all others, taking its rightful place (so he said) at the apex of the world's nations.

Millions of deaths, more millions of injuries, landscapes changed from farm and forest to wastelands of pits and trenches, all were Willy's way of revenging himself on his mother and her homeland.

From his understanding of his parental inheritances—from his resentment of his mother, his contempt for her, his belief that his father would have been a great man if not for her—came not only his determination to be paramount in the world, but also that sense of great destiny just missed which gripped Germany between the wars and precipitated Hitler's monomania.

Exactly when was the decisive moment that ensured disaster would follow? It may have been when the handsome young crown prince went walking on the hills near Balmoral with the bright, witty, entertaining fourteen-year-old princess and proposed to her. For how could their marriage have done anything but bring forth an Anglophobe determined to revenge the wrongs he was sure he'd suffered? Given the nature of the Prussian court, given the nature of the English princess, it is hard to imagine how their marriage— so satisfying to each other despite political disappointments— could have been anything but a train wreck for the whole world in the end.

You Shot Whom?

On July 11, 1804, two men met on the field of honor.
They exchanged shots.
One fell to the ground.
The other fell from grace.

HAMILTON AND BURR

WEEHAWKEN, NEW JERSEY, 1804

Brian M. Thomsen

The One Who Couldn't Keep His Mouth Shut

Alexander Hamilton was born out of wedlock on the island of Nevis in 1755. Despite this inauspicious beginning, the young man made his way to New York in 1772, where he attended Kings College and became active in the local militia in opposition to the Crown.

In March of 1777 he ascended to the rank of aide-de-camp to George Washington, a position he held until 1781, when he was given his own command of a battalion at Yorktown, where he took part in the final battle of the American Revolution.

From the war he moved back to New York to a career in law and politics. He eventually helped establish the Bank of New York, which then led to his election to the state legislature and on to the Continental Congress, where he helped to author the now-famous Federalist Papers, which laid the groundwork for the Constitution of the United States.

He accepted a post as secretary of the treasury in the Washington administration and immediately worked toward those sorts of reforms that would lead to a republic that did not separate the national interest from the interests of those who were among her most economically successful citizens.

Hamilton always considered himself a favorite of Washington's and plotted to eventually succeed him. He even rewrote part of Washington's farewell address to stress those Federalist issues most important to his own platforms and those of his party. A self-promoting war hero, he considered himself an obvious choice.

Others disagreed.

Many found Hamilton priggish and abrasive, and his wrong-side-of-the-sheets birth as well as numerous scandals of his own making more than ensured that he would never ascend to the presidency— which in Hamilton's mind did not necessarily preclude him from still running things.

Indeed he called things as he saw them and had no hesitation about sharing his thoughts about politics and other matters with as many people as he came in contact with, which led to more than a few problems. Eventually his gossiping evolved into very public personal attacks on his opponents, including John Adams, who was running for reelection for the presidency.

It was only a matter of time before his venomous tongue got him into really big trouble.

The One Who Wouldn't Leave Well Enough Alone

Aaron Burr was born in Newark, New Jersey, in 1756, the grandson of legendary "Great Awakening" minister Jonathan Edwards. He graduated from Princeton at the age of sixteen and began legal studies. His practice of law was interrupted by the coming of the American Revolution, where he served valiantly under both Benedict Arnold and George Washington (who, it is alleged, ceased to trust him after an occasion when Washington discovered him rifling through his correspondence before the general had even read it yet).

After the war he returned to his legal practice, entering politics and eventually rising to the offices of both state attorney general and eventually U.S. senator.

Burr was a masterful politician who knew how to manipulate the political machine at both the local and national levels, usually to his own benefit, as evidenced by his manipulation of the electoral process, which resulted in his blocking John Adams's bid for reelection as well as his own securing of the vice presidency in the administration of Thomas Jefferson, despite the new president's personal wariness and distrust of him.

Burr was efficient and knew how to get things done politically, and his number-one priority was simple—Aaron Burr looked out for Aaron Burr.

And it was only a matter of time before someone made public the ruthlessness of his nature, which only his friends and competitors were aware of.

The Disagreements

The discord between the two men had been constant since both had come to prominence and was probably not helped by the differences in their birth and manner—Hamilton the priggish bastard with airs, Burr the roguish gentleman with a penchant for slyness—nor by their common experience as officers under Washington during the Revolution.

While Hamilton was picked by Washington to be the first secretary of the treasury, Burr won his U.S. Senate seat over
Hamilton's father-in-law, and from that point on Hamilton was
hell-bent on making sure that Burr was kept in check—from
throwing his New York support behind Burr's opponent (John Jay)
in a gubernatorial race to his veto of Burr's appointment as quar-
termaster general in the U.S. Army. Hamilton even went so far as
to support Jefferson in the presidential race, despite the fact that
Jefferson's democratic philosophy was in diametric opposition to
Hamilton's own conservative way of thinking. Such matters,
though frustrating to Burr, had to be viewed by him as pure politics and, in point of fact, were similar to actions that he himself
had taken on numerous occasions.

Hamilton, however, was not content with thwarting his opponent politically—he demanded the moral high ground as well,
questioning the man's morals and integrity, often referring to him
as Cataline, the infamous and degenerately traitorous Roman
politician, all along claiming that he was merely protecting the
public good from Burr, loudly stating, "I feel it is a religious duty
to oppose his career." When Burr decided to try another run at the
governorship of New York (probably as a prelude to a run for the
presidency), Hamilton increased his attacks against the former vice
president with poisonous comments on his ethics and morality as
well as his private life, despite the fact that Hamilton himself was
guilty of more than a few sexual indiscretions.

It is even alleged that Hamilton in private meetings hinted that
Burr might have performed unnatural acts with his own daughter
and that Burr "was a dangerous man who ought not to be trusted
with the reins of government."

When these allegations started to appear in print, Burr had no choice but to demand a retraction and apology from Hamilton, who weaseled around the matter in a lawyerly way, refusing to refute his statements or take responsibility for them, while also refusing to apologize or even recognize the situation required clarification.

Faced with a recalcitrant Hamilton having poisoned the waters of public opinion against him, Burr was left with no choice but to protect his "good name" and political career, and challenge Hamilton to a duel.

The Duel

Burr prepared for the duel by practicing his marksmanship.

Hamilton prepared for the duel by telling as many of his and Burr's mutual acquaintances that he bore no ill will toward the vice president and that he intended to withhold fire during the duel. He still did not, it must be noted, offer a recant, refutation, or apology for the remarks attributed to him that were the cause for the disagreement.

The actual accounts of the duel's details vary. What is agreed on is that both parties at some point fired their pistols. Burr's party claimed that Hamilton fired first, missed, and Burr returned fire, hitting and mortally wounding the former secretary of the treasury. Hamilton's party disagreed, claiming that Hamilton's gun either misfired or went off when he was hit by Burr's shot. No matter which actually occurred, the outcome was beyond dispute—both pistols were fired and one of the participants was soon dead.

Burr was allowed to serve out the rest of his term as vice president, but he soon fell into greater disrepute when he was connected to a conspiracy and was later tried for treason. Not even he, the master of politics that he was, could regain the public's good graces and the trust of his colleagues after having killed Hamilton.

An apology would have saved Hamilton's life.

A shot to wound rather than a shot to kill would have saved Burr's political future.

As a result both men suffered for their failing to do the right thing, and as a result the duel in Weehawken sealed the fate of two of America's founding fathers.

You Invaded Where?

We tend to encourage ambition . . . until someone fails. And in this case one of the greatest generals of all times certainly managed to fail on a level most lesser mortals can't even contemplate.

NAPOLEON BONAPARTE

RUSSIA, 1812

Bill Fawcett

The invasion of Russia, ruled by Tsar Alexander (the title is derived from the Roman emperor's rank of Caesar, and the same root from which the Prussian title kaiser is derived), was perhaps the worst mistake in the emperor of France's career. On the tactical level and, indeed, the grand tactical level, Napoleon was a genius almost without peer. But in this one case he made a strategic blunder, three actually, and all of his genius could not save him from the consequences.

In June of 1812 Napoleon was the undisputed master of all continental Europe. The only enemy that remained unconquered was the British, and the only other nation not totally under his thumb, either occupied or battered into submission, was Russia. This is not to say the Russian army had distinguished itself to date. The Russian Empire was in the far side of Europe, literally months of marching away from France. It was for some time even a valuable ally, if a strange one, for republican France.

So why did Napoleon invade?

Basically, England made him do it. Having failed miserably to gain control of the English Channel even long enough to cross with a single army, which was all the conquest would have taken, Napoleon turned to economic warfare. England was an industrial giant but poor in resources; it lived by trade and selling the goods manufactured in its factories and mills. If the emperor could undermine the English economy, the nation was itself too small and weak to be any further threat. Simply put, if the British economy could be crippled, the nation could no longer afford to maintain the largest and most expensive fleet in the world.

All trade between continental Europe and England was banned by imperial decree. With no markets, the English economy would collapse. This was called the Continental System. The problem was that the merchants on the continent who had been importing and shipping goods to England and the colonies would also be impoverished, sometimes whole coastal cities plunged into instant depression. There was, needless to say, a lot of internal resistance even in France itself. In the occupied nations, such as Prussia and Denmark, smuggling became the order of the day. Finally there was Russia, whose ports connected to roads leading into all of Europe and who could least afford the damage this new Continental System would do to its still weak economy. Even after being pressured to sign onto this Continental System, Russia simply ignored it. As much as for ego, and to open the entire Orient to his armies, Napoleon invaded Russia in an effort to bankrupt Britain.

So the first decision that sealed Napoleon's fate was to invade Russia.

After all, much more powerful nations, such as Austria, had been conquered, some more than once. What made Russia so different? To start with, Russia is big. Then there is the small matter of roads, small because effectively, unlike the rest of Europe, there really weren't any. Finally it was empty, much less densely populated than the rest of Europe. To an army that "lived off the land" and numbered hundreds of thousands, these were severe problems. But at first things went well. Fortresses and cities fell, and it was still summer.

Finally able to bring the Russian army, which had retreated ahead of him for months, to battle at Borodino, Napoleon won, driving the Russian army from the field and leaving the roads to Moscow open. A few days later, his army entered Moscow. Okay, he had their capital—well, the winter capital anyhow—and largest city. So Napoleon waited for the delegation to determine the terms of the new treaty he would impose on a conquered Russia. And that was Napoleon's other blunder, he waited. And waited, and waited until the last minute.

The army was tired, and Moscow was large enough to house it all comfortably, even after a part of the city burned. There the French sat for weeks, awaiting a response to the offers sent to the tsar in St. Petersburg. It wasn't until late in the fall that Napoleon accepted the fact that no surrender was coming.

Just sitting in Moscow for all that time was the second decision that led to Napoleon's fall.

Finally, with food getting scarce and winter approaching, Napoleon reluctantly accepted the inevitable and led his army back toward the Vistula River and friendly Poland. The original plan was to march back by a different and more southern route than the one the army had entered on. This had the advantage of taking it through new areas in which to forage for food and fodder. But one nasty engagement, the movement of the Russian forces, and the desire to add to his retreating army the tens of thousands of men stationed at the depots and cities along his route, caused Napoleon to decide to retreat along the same route he had entered Russia by months earlier.

This change of route was the third mistake, and perhaps the worst. It sealed the Grand Army's fate.

The problem was that this route had already been not only stripped bare by both his and the retreating Russian armies when he entered, but that what little remained was ordered burned by Kutusov, the Russian commander. The lack of food, combined with an early and fierce winter, turned most of the still-undefeated French army into a mass of struggling fugitives. The majority of the more than half million soldiers who had so triumphantly marched into Russia months before were lost. Units that began the war with thousands of men in them disappeared entirely. Napoleon hurried back to France to raise and train a new army, but too many experienced officers and men were lost. Worse yet, those whom the emperor had dominated through intimidation lost their fear. They united to defeat this last army at Dresden the next May, 1813. A few months later Napoleon Bonaparte was in exile on Elba. Three decisions made a thousand miles away in Russia did more than anything else to put him there. He would briefly return to power, but that is another tale of another fateful decision.

You Gave Command to Whom?

Sometimes a lot of history is the result of putting the right man in the right job. Or in the case of Napoleon, the wrong man in that job. This is the tale of two marshals of France and why Napoleon lost the Battle of Waterloo.

NAPOLEON

WATERLOO, 1815

Bill Fawcett

The highest military position, over general officers even, is the rank of marshal, which was a holdover from the monarchy and was resurrected by Napoleon when he made himself emperor of France in 1804. In total, he appointed twenty-six marshals who had or did actively command troops. These appointments varied from being a reward for past service to the Revolution to recognition of their position in command of the newly conceived corps. The new formation, the corps (which was really a small army capable of fighting by itself and even holding much larger numbers of opponents in place for a short time), was why there was a need for marshals. Each corp had several divisions, and the title "general" still referred to "general de division" from the days when an overall commander simply gathered the divisions, arrayed them and sent them forward into battle. There was a need for an officer clearly above the general, hence the marshals.

There are endless books about the marshals and debates over how competent or incompetent they were. Here we are concerned with the two men Napoleon considered to command France's only real field army under him. This is important because of a mundane and almost humorous (unless you have had them) ailment that Napoleon suffered from—piles, or, in the modern medical terminology, hemorrhoids. He spent a good deal of the battle of Waterloo sitting in pain, likely less than clearheaded and not very mobile, which makes his decision as to whom to appoint to actually command the army at Waterloo most important. More so when you realize how close the French came to winning that battle, which Wellington described as "a near run thing."

The two men Napoleon says he considered for the field command were Marshal Joachim Ney, "the Bravest of the Brave," and Louis-Nicholas Davout, known as the Iron Marshal. These were two very different men, who fought in very different ways.

Joachim Ney was born in 1769 and was the second son of a barrel cooper (his father made barrels; remember this is France and wine is fermented in barrels). His father had fought in the Seven Years War but had returned to Lorraine near the border with the German states to raise a family afterward. Ney was educated to become a notary, which in those times enabled him to advance, after many years, to the not very august position of very minor bureaucrat overseeing forges and mines. Two years before the Revolution (France's, not the U.S. colonial one) the young man looked at what his future would hold and enlisted as a hussar in the Royal Cavalry. Being of common birth, there was little chance he could advance far in the ranks. It took him four more years to gain his first promotion to corporal. Then came the

Revolution and birth ceased to control rank. Three years later Joachim Ney was a lieutenant and aide-de-camp for a series of generals. He was favored by one man who was the Revolution's most successful early general, Jean-Victor Moreau. Fortunately for Ney this friendship faded due to distance and the press of war. Moreau was never convicted—due to his prestige a public trial was out of the question—but it is known that he was part of a plot to assassinate Napoleon during his 1804 inauguration. Moving up in the ranks because of the large numbers of officers lost, many to the guillotine rather than enemy action, the young officer Ney married the daughter of a rich official who was the protégé of Napoleon's future empress, Josephine.

His close personal relationship with Josephine helped, along with a good reputation and popularity among the men he commanded, to gain Ney a position under Napoleon commanding the Sixth Corps, who were assembled on the coast in preparation for the invasion of England, which the Battle of Trafalgar made impossible. From 1805 to 1811 Ney served with courage, if occasional lassitude, in moving his corp throughout central Europe. He continued to command during Napoleon's ill-fated invasion of Russia in 1812. This was a life-changing event for the still-young marshal. The winter retreat was epic and disastrous, with much of the core of Napoleon's Grand Army being lost. Ney commanded the rear guard, and did so magnificently. His command started with several thousand men, and when it was the last of the army to cross the Vistula back into Poland, the hundreds remaining were still forming their ranks and marching as a unit when virtually all of the rest of the survivors of the retreat had degenerated into a formless mob of fugitives. During this retreat the strain was so great that the marshal's famous red hair turned white. Soon, after the Battle of Nations, Napoleon abdicated and Ney retained position under the restored monarchy.

Unlike Ney, Louis-Nicholas Davout was born into a Burgundian family whose nobility and tradition of military service went back to the Crusades. The young Davout was accepted into the prestigious Royal Champagne Cavalry Regiment, where he proceeded to immediately get into trouble for supporting the Revolution that had begun to sweep across France. He was even imprisoned for attending a revolutionary meeting in Paris without bothering to ask for a leave. After being freed the young man found he had little to do, not being trusted by his royalist superiors, and with good reason. He married during this period of enforced boredom. (It was a disaster, but that was a purely personal blunder.)

Finally, the Revolution began forming its own cavalry units, and his jail time and reputation protected the young Davout from the shortening by a head that most of the ancien régime officers who stayed in France were subjected to. He rose quickly from being elected to commanding a battalion to general of the brigade within a year. Under Napoleon, Louis Davout commanded the Third Corps, the largest corp in the army, for almost a decade. He was a hard taskmaster, not so much loved as respected, but his Third Corps twice (Ausdadt and Austerlitz) fought to a standstill Allied armies that greatly outnumbered them.

So now fast-forward to 1812.

Wars have been won and lost. The impetuous Ney is a marshal of France sworn to serve the king and Davout is a prisoner of war.

Napoleon escapes from Elba and lands in France. Davout, now freed, hurries to his side. Ney, in the court of Louis XVIII, promises to bring his former emperor to the king in a "cage." By the time his infantry division faces Napoleon, Ney has had a change of heart, and probably realizes that all his soldiers were likely to go over to Napoleon in any case. All of those sent with earlier generals had. On bended knee, and to the cheers of the army, he asks Napoleon to forgive and accept him. As charismatic and popular as ever, Ney enters Paris, the king long gone, at Napoleon's side a few days later.

So here was the choice: the popular hero or the respected and loyal taskmaster?

There are two key positions the returned emperor has to fill with a marshal. One is commander of the army, his number two in effect. The other is to command Paris and its garrison. Controlling Paris meant ruling France, and losing Paris would mean he had lost control of the bureaucracy who controlled little things like money, food, and recruits. He had to have a trusted and competent man to run Paris, and over Davout's protests, Napoleon put Davout in command of the city, not the army. Command of the Reinstituted Grand Army went to Marshal Ney, whose popularity would help sway any units still unsure whom to support. In effect he took the most popular man, who was a worn but competent corp commander, and left behind in Paris the man most proven in battle against all odds and who was the only other man in France who had commanded anywhere near the size of the army they were fielding. Napoleon had a plan that would have worked. If Napoleon had been fully capable of commanding the army, it did not matter who passed in his orders. But as it turned out, he wasn't.

Louis-Nicholas Davout said it himself. He warned Napoleon that if he was victorious, Paris would be his, but if the emperor was defeated, no man could hold the city for him. Napoleon ignored the advice and marched to, well, his Waterloo. Ney was brave and his personal courage inspired the French cavalry to attack the British squares for literally hours, ignoring severe casualties until they could no longer even move toward the squares of bristling bayonets at a slow walk. Then again Ney ordered that first charge by all the cavalry in the army, to Napoleon's recorded dismay, when he mistook the withdrawal of a few British battalions back over a hill for the start of a full retreat. Still, even then it almost worked. The entire day of the battle the entire French army attacked straight at the British in a reflection of Ney's own brash, aggressive manner while Napoleon, the master of the flanking maneuver, sat far behind the battlefield too ill and in too much pain to do more.

Would Davout have fought Waterloo differently? That seems likely. He was most certainly a very different type of commander. His record in past battles was one of efficient and reasoned leadership. Steady where Ney was impulsive, efficient more than brave. Would just a few moments of calmer consideration and calculated movement have made a difference? Wellington won the Battle of Waterloo literally by a matter of minutes, and the massed musket fire of a few thousand tired, thirsty men in the 52nd and the Foot Guards stopped the French Old Guard's desperate columns from splitting their center, an action that would almost certainly have routed the badly depleted and exhausted British and Dutch. If there had been even a few thousand heavy cavalry remaining to accompany them, the British would have been unable to form line and their firepower would have been seriously diminished. But there weren't.

Ney was executed by a suitably, in the king's opinion, betrayed Louis. Davout eventually was made minister of war and reformed the French army. If Napoleon had given his most efficient Iron Marshal command of his army at Waterloo . . . ?

You Wore What?

Clothes make the man. Or in this case a misplaced sense of macho and style made all the difference. For want of a scarf, the kingdom was lost.

WILLIAM HENRY HARRISON
WASHINGTON, D.C., 1840

Brian M. Thomsen

William Henry Harrison was a hero of the War of 1812, the leader of the American Army of the Northwest credited with killing Tecumseh and smashing his confederacy, which many believed forced the British to abandon their holdings in the American Northwest. He also served in both houses of Congress, and was setting his sights on the White House.

The year was 1840, and Harrison had deftly manuevered himself into the role of favorite presidential candidate for the Whig party. A true successor to the popular man-of-action legacy of the party as personified best by Andrew "Old Hickory" Jackson, he had positioned himself as part war hero and part farmer (despite his Virginia aristocrat roots) with a log cabin legacy and a hankering for hard cider. He and his supporters even came up with a slogan that has entered the annals of all-time memorable political campaigns; "Tippecanoe and Tyler too" was an alliterative stroke of genius that linked Harrison's quasi-distinguished war record as the "hero" of the Battle of Tippecanoe with the name of his running mate in a slogan that politically meant nothing but at the same time kept the candidates' identities front and center. Indeed Harrison's entire campaign followed suit with massive, hard-drinking rallies to support his candidacy, with an abundance of political doodads, emblems, and party favors of log cabins, buck-skin balls, and patriotic streamers with a notable lack of solid pub-lic policy and substance.

Harrison had set his sights on defeating the incumbent presi-dent, Martin Van Buren, the so-called Little Magician of Kinderhook, with a man's man-of-action campaign. He became the backwoods war hero he had enacted for the campaign, and that was whom the American people wanted for president.

He was also the candidate the political fixers wanted as well. This was the dawning of party politics as controlled by backroom bosses in smoke-filled rooms. The Whig party advocated a weak presidency with the government supported primarily by a strong Congress. In many ways the president, in their opinions, was pri-marily a figurehead, and who better for the presidential mantle than a candidate whose entire platform consisted of image and hype with very little substance or policy?

And it worked!

With 82 percent of the eligible populace voting, Harrison locked up 53 percent of the popular vote, and an overwhelming majority in the electoral college.

William Henry Harrison was victorious . . . and he was also exhausted.

The road to the White House had been rugged, and the candi-date had given his all in hard-drinking, glad-handing, in-the-trenches campaigning, and even though he contended "I am not the old man on crutches nor the imbecile they say I am," he was nonetheless sixty-five-plus years old and hadn't really been paying attention to his health, leaving him quite drained, exhausted, and frail once the election was over.

Still the president-elect realized that it was the projected image that had won him the office, and he swore to himself that he would do his darnedest to maintain it.

The American people had not elected a frail old man.

They had elected a robust and rollicking war hero, and that was whom they were going to see take the oath of office.

Inauguration Day arrived, and with it a bout of bad weather. It was rainy, and when it wasn't actually raining it was cold and damp.

But William Henry Harrison knew that first impressions counted, and this was his first opportunity to impress the American people as their new president. So, in an effort to show his fearlessness against the elements, the new president removed his hat and his coat despite the inclement weather, and proceeded to deliver one of the longest inaugural addresses in the history of the presidency.

He got an overwhelming ovation.

He also got a cold.

By the time he arrived at the presidential residence at 1600 Pennsylvania Avenue, he was completely worn-out and beset by chills, with a fever on the way. He ordered an alcohol rub and promptly went to bed.

The next day, however, there were favors to repay, and the White House was besieged by job seekers all hoping to receive some presidential appointment in exchange for all of their hard work. Harrison met with them, sometimes around the clock, and as he continued to strengthen his political ties, his own health deteriorated.

The Inauguration Day cold blossomed with every passing, exhausting day and in no time at all was a full-blown case of pneumonia.

Exactly one month after Harrison's fearless display of heartiness and fortitude, the new president was pronounced dead from his respiratory infection.

The brave war hero was no match for the infection, nor was the actually frail old man a worthy opponent for the most basic common cold or a bit of chill and dampness in the air.

The bravado of the candidate resulted in the shortest presidency in American history.

You Set Loose What?

Some mistakes end in horrible consequences. Others go unnoticed. But most noteworthy are those mistakes that continue to reverberate and annoy millions for more than a century.

THOMAS AUSTIN AND THE GOVERNORS OF AUSTRALIA

AUSTRALIA, 1859

Keith R. A. DeCandido

Rabbits were introduced modestly to the continent of Australia when it became a dumping ground for British convicts in the eighteenth century. The First Fleet's manifest in 1788 included one stallion, three mares, three colts, two bulls, five cows, twenty-nine sheep, nineteen goats, forty-nine hogs, twenty-five pigs, eighteen turkeys, twenty-nine geese, thirty-five ducks, one hundred twenty-two fowls, eighty-seven chickens—and five rabbits. More were brought to Sydney in 1791 aboard the *Gorgon* via South Africa, and others no doubt came in that have since gone unaccounted for.

These and other rabbits that were imported did not cause any major difficulties—at first. In the early part of the nineteenth century, rabbits were introduced to New South Wales, Tasmania, and even to their own island—a small island off Wilson's Promontory was dubbed Rabbit Island since, according to accounts, two black-furred rabbits were left there by what one sailor called "a praise-worthy sealer," and proceeded to overrun the island. By 1846, according to one account, whalers used to go to Rabbit Island for sport and food. Attempts were even made to breed them.

The dam broke in December 1859, thanks to an English tenant farmer named Thomas Austin of Barwon Park, Winchelsea, near Geelong. Austin had made a fortune in Australia and wished to have hunts in his new home, as did several of his fellow members of the upper crust. He would not lower himself to using the near-by Tasmanian rabbits, nor any of the other local strains that had been developed in the last seventy years. Instead, he wrote to his brother and had him send down seventy-two partridges, five hares, and twenty-four English wild rabbits. Austin's hunting parties proved immensely popular to the British men who were starved for "proper" hunts.

The first hunting party took place on Christmas Day, 1859, which was apropos, since releasing those twenty-four rabbits proved to be a perpetual "gift" to the Australian ecosystem. The initial two dozen bred like mad. In 1867, *The Field* reported a kill near Barwon Park of over fourteen thousand rabbits, all descendants of those first two dozen. That same year, in a move that caused no end of hindsight-induced wincing, Austin was awarded a medal by the Acclimatisation Society for his successful introduction of the rabbit to Australia.

"Successful," in this case, is a relative term. Rabbits have no natural predator in Australia, nor were there any local diseases that would claim them. Australia being an island, no such diseases were likely to be introduced. Meanwhile, they ate any greenery they could sink their teeth into, often at the expense of the native sheep, cattle, and other livestock. They bred like, well, rabbits, and soon Australia was covered in a gray, furry carpet.

Austin was not the only one not to think through the consequences. In 1854, Albrecht Feez of New England, New South Wales, turned out rabbits he had with him because no one would buy them. By 1865, he had been advised never to appear in New England again, as his rabbits had multiplied such that they were destroying the best land in the area.

The spread of the rabbits was as much due to lethargy as anything. The traditional methods of restraining livestock, wire fencing or stone walls, proved woefully ineffective; the rabbits would simply climb the fence or dig underneath. The only effective means—for example, six-foot-high walls and trenches lined with broken glass and sharp metal—were prohibitively expensive.

Many locals welcomed the rabbits at first. In 1866, landowners begged the government to legislate to protect the rabbits, as they were being attacked by those who disliked having their crops eaten by rampaging hordes of bunnies. By 1872, those same landowners were begging even more fervently for legislation to make the destruction of rabbits compulsory.

By the turn of the century, extraordinary measures were required. In 1907, the Western Australian No. 1 Rabbit Proof Fence was completed. It stretched over eleven hundred miles— a distance twice the length of Great Britain—from Starvation Boat Harbor on the south coast to a point near Cape Keraudren on the northwest coast. Guarded by riders on camels, the fence was constructed in an attempt to prevent the rabbits from literally eating their way across Australia. Unfortunately, such a massive fence proved impossible to maintain, and it proved ultimately ineffective.

Every attempt was made to control the rabbit plague—for they were now considered such—whether by gun, trap, poison, or attack by ferret, but nothing worked for long or in any practically useful numbers. The government offered a reward of twenty-five thousand pounds to anyone who could come up with a solution. Sadly, this mostly brought out the greedy fanatics. In the 1890s, a gentleman named W. Rodier had tried an odd sort of eugenics program in which he would kill *only* does, leaving the bucks alive, on the theory that the smaller supply of females would force the males to gang up on them and make them less likely to reproduce. Years of failure for this to in any way change things did not deter Rodier, who fervently believed in his disastrous system until he died in the 1930s. Adrian Loir, the nephew of the famous Dr. Louis Pasteur, suggested spreading a chicken cholera among the rabbits; chicken farmers pointed out the obvious danger to their chickens in such a solution.

A strain of myxomatosis was discovered to be killing rabbits in California in the 1930s. Dame Jean Macnamara attempted to introduce myxomatosis to Australia, which met with surprising resistance and difficulty, though a program of infection finally came to pass. By 1959, the hundredth anniversary of Austin's ill-advised importing, the myxomatosis had severely curtailed the rabbit population, but it turned out to be only a temporary solution, as the rabbits eventually developed an immunity.

In the mid-1990s, a Rabbit Calicivirus Disease was launched, which dropped the rabbit populations in the more arid parts of Australia by 95 percent. It is still only a partial measure, but a necessary one. In 1997, rabbits cost Australia over $1 billion per year, approximately $600,000 of that in agricultural costs alone. Each attempt to curtail the rabbit infestation seems only to slow them down briefly. Thomas Austin's desire for hunting game has reduced an entire continent to an island full of Elmer Fudds continually confounded by a rampaging horde of Bugs Bunnies.

You Lost What?

The American Civil War is considered one of the first modern wars. Troops used breech-loading weapons, and rapid-firing Gatling guns appeared, along with ironclad warships and turrets. It is refreshing to note that a simple, old-fashioned mistake may have changed the course of the whole conflict.

ROBERT E. LEE AND GENERAL GEORGE B. McCLELLAN
ANTIETAM, 1862

Brian M. Thomsen

Special orders do upset us . . .

The Civil War was being fought brother against brother, and nowhere was this more prevalent than among the cadre of elite officers who made up the high command for both the Union and the Confederate forces. In many cases these commanders were previously classmates or at least fellow alumni at the honored United States Military Academy at West Point, and they were now forced to sue their shared educations and trainings against one another on the battlefields of Maryland, Virginia and the Carolinas.

Robert E. Lee had graduated at the head of his class and was considered by everyone in the military to be the epitome of what it meant to be an officer and a gentleman, and it was with a heavy heart that he resigned his commission in the army of the United States of America to accept the leadership of the army of the rebelling Confederate States of America. By following the allegiances of the place of his birth he knew that he would be, like the country itself, torn asunder by having to do battle with the brothers he had formerly led into combat.

George B. McClellan, heir to a Philadelphia fortune, West Point graduate (second in his class), decorated veteran of the Mexican War, and successful businessman, was heralded as "the Young Napoleon" who would put the Confederacy in its place and bring to a swift end the rebellion that had occurred after the South had fired on Fort Sumter, when he was appointed as commander of the Union's Army of the Potomac. With his experience, enthusiasm, and intelligence, a quick victory was ensured in the minds of his supporters (and his own) and would lay the groundwork for a run to the White House in the upcoming presidential election.

There was no mistaking his qualifications. He was a master strategist and a self-assured leader; but unfortunately he also tended to overthink problems and draft scenarios that were overly complicated to execute under the fog of war, and as a result the swift and sure victory he had guaranteed was very slow in coming.

The delays codified certain doubts in Washington, which resulted in a major loss of face and support at the high command, which George quickly wrote off as the work of his political rivals, opponents, and detractors. More than anything the situation made him even more cautious as he began to fear making a mistake (and the repercussions on his ego and image) more than the battlefield consequences of any mistake itself.

After having been temporarily relieved of his command (and then reinstated) George was itching for a decisive victory over his Confederate nemesis, Robert E. Lee, and the upcoming Battle of

Antietam had the potential to provide him with just such a proving ground.

Robert E. Lee had issued orders for the next phase of his invasion (Army of Northern Virginia Special Order Number 191), which outlined his plans, and had disseminated it to his men, detailing how he was dividing his forces with plans for them to converge on Harpers Ferry and Boonsboro several days hence. George's acquisition of these orders would enable him to predict his opponents' moves, counter them, and outmaneuver them in such a way as to exploit their division, and damage them beyond repair, thus enabling him to realize the quick and decisive victory that was needed to reestablish his reputation.

Unfortunately, Union commanders were not usually on the circulation list for Confederate orders and memos, so it was extremely unlikely that such detailed orders could make their way into George's hands . . . but somehow that was exactly what happened.

Lee's ranks had suffered some recent dissension. Though his subordinate officers, such as Longstreet and Jackson, held Lee in the highest regard in terms of respect (a quality not shared by McClellan and his subordinates), hurt feelings and tactical disagreements about everything from large-scale military planning to the allocation of seized ambulances were beginning to come into play as the Confederate force became worn down by the sheer superior numbers that were being brought to bear against them by the Union forces. Thus dissension led to a certain degree of sloppiness all the way down the line, and privileged communications were not always treated with the heightened security that they required. So when Lee divided his forces and then sent out the message that included the timetable and point of rendezvous, a situation occurred that led to one copy of these orders going astray.

Two soldiers in McClellan's Twenty-seventh Indiana were resting off the roadside and in the woods outside of Frederick when they discovered the remnants of a rebel campsite that had been recently deserted. Among the Confederate castoffs were some rags and busted equipment and three slightly soggy cigars carefully wrapped in some paper.

After examining the cigars carefully and determining that they could be dried out in the sun and thus rendered serviceable (if not as good as new), the soldiers were about to discard their wrinkled wrappings when they noticed some writing on it.

Army of Northern Virginia Special Order Number 191

Both of them realized that this wrapping was indeed more important than the cigars, and hustled their way back to the command center so that the recently acquired Confederate missive could be moved up the chain of command to McClellan. This information could allow him to direct his forces to pursue the split forces of Lee, who were already behind in their tactical schedule.

McClellan was apprehensive about this unexpected good fortune. Were these orders real? Were they accurate? Could this be a trap? Even though time was of the essence, the West Point graduate and self-appointed military genius of the Union forces decided to review the situation from all angles before concluding that it would indeed be beneficial to take advantage of the allegedly divided forces of his Confederate counterpart, and immediately put in motion a plan to do so.

That plan resulted in the Battle of Antietam, the single bloodiest day in U.S. military history, when McClellan's forces engaged with Lee's.

Lee was outnumbered, but McClellan was overly cautious and on numerous occasions slow to react to changes in circumstance. As a result the Union suffered over twelve thousand casualties, as compared to slightly over ten thousand for the Confederates.

Moreover, McClellan was more worried about suffering a defeat than pressing for a victory, and as a result he never fully pressed his numeric superiority against Lee's divided force, as if he believed that Lee's orders were in reality bait for a trap in which an undisclosed Confederate supplementary force might ambush them once they were fully committed to combat.

Even after the battle was over (and victory claimed), McClellan opted to rest and regroup and wait for reinforcements rather than dogging the fleeing Lee and his men and delivering what would surely have been a deathblow to the Confederate forces, which were scattered, vulnerable, and on the run.

McClellan's overcautiousness resulted in a lost opportunity that might have foreshortened the war drastically, and indeed provided the Union general with just the sort of platform of heroism and military genius that he desired to support him in his planned run for the presidency. The self-assured general overthought, overplanned, and, as a result, underperformed. By failing to press an engagement based on victory through attrition (which he and his forces would surely have won), McClellan wasted the golden opportunity that fate had presented him, and this eventually resulted in his removal (once again) from command of the Army of the Potomac.

It was only after the actual battle had passed that Lee recognized how lucky he and his men really were. Carelessness in the issuing and protection of orders and laxity in conduct in the field had almost dealt the Confederate forces a mortal blow. It was only by the clearheadedness of his officers, his own grip on the situation in progress, and no small degree of dumb luck that he and his command survived. Lee was grateful that the gods had smiled on him that day, and renewed his commitment to defend the South with his heart, mind, and soul.

McClellan never regained that command or went on to be elected president (though a lesser student at West Point, Ulysses Simpson Grant, did indeed eventually take his place in command and in the White House), and McClellan spent the latter part of his life blaming others for his misfortune and missed opportunities. His memoirs are a model of self-aggrandizement, rewritten history, and self-deception.

You Taught Them What?

There is nothing like training your enemies to fight you. And certainly we have modern examples. It is almost consoling to see that this particular mistake is not a new one.

WILLIAM CLARKE QUANTRILL
KANSAS AND MISSOURI, 1863

Brian M. Thomsen

With the coming of the Civil War neighboring states soon found themselves to be the bloody battlegrounds for a conflict that was only partially based on high ideals such as states' rights, federalism, and the ever-popular rights of man. Nowhere was it more ambiguous than in the western territories and in the bordering states of Kansas and Missouri, where the lack of a major military presence for either side did little to diminish the carnage and collateral damage that went hand in hand with a time of war.

Many of the Southern/Confederate sympathizers looked for an outlet for their patriotic fervor closer to home rather than enlisting for duty in the predominantly eastern-based military service, and as a result, formed vigilante bands of marauders who would cross state lines to wreak havoc on pro-Union communities and abolitionist enclaves.

These bands became known as bushwhackers, and one of their most famous and successful leaders was William Clarke Quantrill.

Quantrill realized that the war would not be won by military engagements alone. Support and supplies needed to be disrupted as well, and the way to accomplish this was through fear. Quantrill and his men targeted Union sympathizers, executing them on the spot, burning their homes and farms as a message to anyone who even wanted to consider not supporting the Confederacy. They also robbed mail coaches, supply trains, and occasionally banks to divert Union supplies (as well as finance their own actions with a little booty set aside as a reward for their self-styled patriotism).

Quantrill taught his men the basics of guerrilla warfare while sermonizing about the justification for their extreme actions.

Not all Southerners, however, agreed with Quantrill's methods. Some were even appalled by their actions, and initially the public stance of the Confederacy was one of condemnation, with accusations of savagery and uncivilized behavior that would not be tolerated.

However, not even the genteel Southern high command could argue with success and effectiveness, and in August of 1862, after Quantrill's men had engineered a truly successful raid on Independence, Missouri, Quantrill's Raiders were retroactively recognized as part of the Confederate military, and their epony-mous leader was given the rank of captain in the Confederate Partisan Ranger Service.

By this time Quantrill's band had swelled to approximately 450 strong, including such luminary marauders as Bloody Bill Anderson and young Raiders in training such as Coleman Younger, and the James brothers, Frank and Jesse, who carefully studied their captain in an effort to master their craft, while also exulting in the excitement and ill-gotten gains that went hand in hand with the guerrilla lifestyle.

Success led to further savagery as the Raiders continued to push the envelope in terms of acceptable military tactics.

Their authorization/endorsement by the Confederate powers wound up being relatively short-lived.

On August 21, 1863, Quantrill and his men staged a raid on the pro-abolitionist town of Lawrence, Kansas. In less than three hours they slaughtered in cold blood close to two hundred men and boys, the captain having ordered them to kill every male capable of firing a gun. They pillaged the town and burned to the ground anything they left behind.

Once again they proved to be an embarrassment to the powers that be, which sent orders for them to desist in their lawless and savage behavior—but the order fell on deaf ears. Quantrill and his men had grown accustomed to disregarding the pleasantries of society like "law" and "civilized behavior," and for as long as they considered their work to be effective, they vowed to continue their actions for the overall good of the Confederacy, as well as their own personal amusement and enrichment.

And so they did, until the force gradually began to disband in late 1864, whether out of a sense of the inevitable defeat of the South or from a mixture of boredom and homesickness. Some continued to function as guerrillas in smaller bands until the surrender at Appomattox Courthouse, while others attempted to continue to wage the war well after, refusing to accept that the Confederacy was now a lost cause.

Still others journeyed home to their farms and readied themselves for their postwar careers, utilizing the education and enlightenment that their service to the cause had afforded them.

Coleman Younger and Frank and Jesse James fell into this category, and no sooner was the surrender signed than the three enlisted the help of several relatives to form their own gang and set about the civilian career of robbing the U.S. mail and banks.

From an ethical standpoint, these students of Quantrill had rationalized that even though the South had been defeated, there was no reason not to continue their guerrilla resistance against Union banks and commercial enterprises (such as the postal service wagons and the railroads). Indeed, their actions were their patriotic duty, not to mention a neat and tidy way of providing a comfortable existence for themselves and their loved ones.

Other Confederate veterans initially rationalized their behavior as just deserts rendered unto the Damn Yankees, and indeed the James and Younger gang was soon lionized as being more akin to Robin Hood than bank robbers (though there is no evidence that they ever distributed their purloined booty to charitable causes) by the sympathetic media, who were desperately searching for folk heroes to alleviate the pervasive oppression of the lost cause. But eventually this support waned to just their family and friends.

The problem was simple.

Outlaws and illegal behavior were just not acceptable for everyday society, and allowances that were made for wartime behavior out of feelings of desperation and vengeance really didn't have a place in the peacetime Great Plains—not to mention that the robbing of banks was not as condonable an action when your own money was involved.

Unfortunately the boys had learned their craft too well. Their military service had provided them with the education, and it was now up to them to use it. And they did, for the fun of it, for profit, and for the lost cause, right up to the times of Cole's and Jesse's deaths at the hands of other similar craftsmen and professional hired killers who wore the stars of office granted to them by the same powers that be who had condoned their actions when it was advantageous for them to do so back in the war so many years ago.

Quantrill's Raiders went from a military force to a gang, one in which many of the next decade's most notorious outlaws had learned their trade.

You Sent Them Out in What?

Sometimes any plan is likely to sink under its own weight. Despite desperation and incredible courage, this is one of those cases.

HORACE LAWSON HUNLEY AND GENERAL P. T. BEAUREGARD
OFF THE CONFEDERATE COASTLINE, 1864

Brian M. Thomsen

The South was in trouble.

The war had dragged on for close to three years, and the Union naval blockade of such ports as Charleston was starving the Confederacy's resupplying efforts from sympathetic nations abroad. The "damage them all you can" strategy of Robert E. Lee was wearing thin, and the North knew that in a war of attrition, they, home to the bastions of manufacturing in the Americas, need only keep up the battering until a starved and battered Confederacy would have to give in.

Though the South had been the first to use the innovation of protective metal plating (the so-called ironclads), the North had already done them one better with a ship that sat less than two feet above the waterline with a single armed turret midship that provided them with a tactical edge beyond mere armament.

Something had to be done to neutralize the Union navy and allow the outmanned and "out-metaled" Confederate forces a fighting chance.

A wealthy New Orleans planter, lawyer, and privateer by the name of Horace Lawson Hunley came up with a plan. What about submarine technology? Though early versions (such as the American Revolution's Turtle) had failed to excite the military masterminds of naval warfare, there was an obvious advantage that could be attained through the use of such a craft. When you were outarmed, you had to be sneaky, and as Brian Hicks and Schuyler Kropf said in their marvelous book *Raising the Hunley*, "For the South the *Hunley* was simply the best response of a nation that was outgunned, outmanned, and outmaneuvered. . . . It was stealth technology in embryo," and it was just the type of equalizer the Confederate navy definitely needed.

Working with two machinists by the names of James McClintock and Baxter Watson, Hunley set about the task of designing a "fishboat" that would be able to get close enough to the Union ships to do their damage before their presence was even recognized.

After numerous experiments and much trial and error, their work came to fruition with a boiler-shaped hull (3½ feet wide, 4 feet tall, and 40 feet long), fitted with stabilizing fins, and a propulsion system that consisted of seven men turning a crank that ran through the ship and turned a propeller in the ship's aft. Snorkels were also fashioned to allow for occasional air replacement (though they never worked properly) and a ballast pump was affixed that could be handled by an eighth crewman who would probably be the commanding officer. A final tweak by Confederate general P. T. Beauregard (commander of forces at Charleston) involving the mounting of a spar torpedo on its bow, and the so-christened *Hunley* submarine was ready for business.

After a couple of disastrous and fatal test runs, on the night of February 17, 1864, the *Hunley* made its successful martial debut and received its baptism under fire. Under the command of Lieutenant George E. Dixon, the sub rammed its torpedo spar into the Union warship *Housatonic,* which was moored outside of Charleston Harbor in plain sight of Sullivan's Island under the command of Captain Charles W. Pickering, and sank her within minutes.

The mission was a success.

The *Hunley* would be the perfect new Confederate terror weapon with which they could reclaim control of their harbor . . . but unfortunately this technological marvel of military malevolence never made it back to port.

Its first mission was also its last.

The problem was that in the haste to take action against the Union forces, a few design flaws were overlooked.

First, there was its weight problem. The ship itself was already heavy, and the addition of a few gallons of seawater from a precipitate leak could very well upset its already tenuous buoyancy and send it on a one-way trip to the ocean floor.

Second, it had a precarious trim and was negatively affected by the slightest changes in weight or movement on board, thus requiring the crew to remain stationary at all times, or risk tipping its delicate and weighted equilibrium to yet another possible one-way trip to the ocean floor.

Third, though the escape hatches worked fine on shore, the weight of the water above, once the submarine had been submerged, made them fairly immobile, affording no real escape and yet again acting as a portal to that classic one-way trip to the ocean floor.

Finally, there was a problem with the mounted spar torpedo that had been suggested by Beauregard. It failed to disengage from the sub once it had made contact with its target (the hull of the *Housatonic*), thus ensuring the destruction of not just its intended prey but the *Hunley* as well.

As they say in medical school, the operation was a success but the patient died, and so did a third complete crew. As the result of a few design flaws, the entire concept of the submarine was shelved for a few more decades before it would once again surface as an instrument of naval military glory.

You're Building What, Where?

Sometimes it is not yet the right time for a good idea. . . .

FERDINAND DE LESSEPS AND FRANCE

PANAMA, 1881

Jody Lynn Nye

Few feats of engineering are as impressive as the Panama Canal. Completed in 1914 by an army of American laborers, it made possible easy and swift passage from the Atlantic Ocean to the Pacific.

It had taken four hundred years for such a thing to become possible. The New World, opened to European exploitation by Spain in 1492 by Christopher Columbus, was a source of gold, new food, spices, goods and, above all, vast lands for the expansionist dreams of the post-Renaissance Old World. Columbus's original plan was to find a means of shortening the trip between Asia and Europe, a transit that at the time was possible only by an arduous overland journey, or by sailing all the way around the Cape of Good Hope at the southern tip of Africa. The explorer Vasco Núñez de Balboa mapped the Pacific coast of Panama in 1513, proving to his Spanish masters how narrow that part of the continent was. At the time all goods from the west had to be transported by mule along a slender road from Peru and Colombia to ships waiting on the eastern edge. A water-filled shortcut through that land would shave 12,000 miles off any sea journey from Europe to the west coast of the Americas or to Asia. In 1524, it was proposed to King Charles V of Spain that a canal across Panama would accomplish that goal.

Plans were drawn up for a canal as early as 1529, and a route was chosen within five years, but growing unrest in Europe stopped the plans from being carried out at that time. Though the idea was occasionally revived by philosophers and great thinkers, it was almost three more centuries before any practical interest was shown in digging a canal through Central America. Some proposals were floated during the early half of the nineteenth century, but what finally brought attention back to easy access to the Pacific coast from Europe was the discovery of gold in California in 1848. Prospectors took ships to Panama, traversed the by-now well-worn road across Panama, and sailed from the west coast north to their goal. Every treasure seeker was now motivated to find a shorter way, and a canal was the obvious answer.

It is no longer widely remembered that there were two possible sites surveyed for the canal: one in Panama and one in Nicaragua. The Nicaraguan site was lower and more level than the route through Panama, but there was no doubt that it was a good deal longer than the forty miles across Panama, so Nicaragua was largely dismissed from serious discussions.

The first company to obtain rights from the Colombian government tried and failed in 1878. Two years later, Ferdinand de Lesseps, famed as the engineer of the recently completed Suez Canal, stepped forward to undertake the project.

In 1880 de Lesseps, who had been French consul to Egypt, was already seventy-five years old. The Suez Canal had taken him ten years to build, from 1859 to 1869. Over 1.5 million workers, many of them Egyptian slaves, were employed to dig the canal, and of those, over 100,000 died from exposure, exertion and disease. The project had begun under the viceroy of Egypt and was completed under Napoleon III. (It's interesting to note that there had been a rudimentary canal that dated from the days of the pharaohs up to the Roman occupation of Egypt, but it had been abandoned and allowed to become derelict when shipping around the Cape of Good Hope became possible.)

The Suez project had originally been delayed because of a belief that the two seas, the Red Sea and the Mediterranean Sea, were of different levels. When this was proved wrong by an international team of engineers, de Lesseps was able to construct a sea-level canal. The resulting channel was a great success, making de Lesseps a national hero. The grand opening in November 1869 was an enormous occasion. Giuseppe Verdi had been commissioned to compose the opera *Aida*, which was performed for the first time in the new Cairo Opera House, also built in celebration of the new canal.

Six years later, de Lesseps let it be known he was ready to tackle the next great canal-building project, "La Grande Tranchee." When he went to backers to ask for money for the Panama enterprise, they were eager to support him.

De Lesseps himself was not an engineer. In 1880 he formed the Compagnie universelle du canal interoceanique with his investors' money. He was certain that he could build a sea-level canal as he had in Egypt. (In fact, flush with the success of the Suez, he had come up with various other insane plans, including linking Moscow and Peking by rail, with Bombay and Paris en route, with a total disregard of geography.) He held a congress in Paris to discuss routes for the project, attended by participants from the United Kingdom, the United States, France, Germany and many other countries. The U.S. Navy in particular had surveyed the area closely and had a lot to say about the difficulty of accomplishing what de Lesseps had in mind. He did not listen to them. He did, however, listen to his own handpicked engineer, Lieutenant Lucien Napoleon-Bonaparte Wyse, who slapped together a plan for him, probably put together out of documents obtained illegally from the United States survey team's reports. Unbelievably, he proposed a tunnel through the mountains, following the line of the existing railway, to avoid having to excavate the path completely. It was pointed out to Wyse that the water course he proposed moving, the Chagres River, was subject to seasonal flooding, like the Nile, and would inundate the tunnel frequently. Thinking on his feet, Wyse then proposed that they would pass the Chagres under the tunnel instead.

Almost unheard, an engineer named Baron Godin de Lepinay proposed an alternate plan that would use a man-made lake as a staging area for ships to pass one another. He was voted down. The congress, packed with de Lesseps's supporters, voted in favor of the plan.

The company seemed to have been in disarray from the beginning. To supply the enterprise with men and goods over the course of the construction, it laid down railroad tracks in Panama, without checking to make certain that the gauge of the existing tracks was the same. In fact, it wasn't. In the company's records were inexplicable purchases, such as an order for 10,000 snow shovels. The project was originally budgeted at $120 million, but the international congress insisted it could not be done for less than $214 million, and even the French engineering board put the cost at $168 million. De Lesseps claimed it could be done in six years. Outside estimates were seven to eight years at a minimum.

De Lesseps's surveyors discovered that their major obstacles were that the Atlantic and Pacific Oceans were indeed of different levels, and that though Panama is narrow, its mountainous spine is the vestige of the Continental Divide that runs unbroken through North and South America. The tides of the Pacific fluctuate far more than those of the Atlantic, between twelve and twenty feet a day, which would have the effect of swamping ships heading westward. A sea-level course was not feasible.

Work began in 1881, but two years later de Lesseps's workforce of 20,000 had yet to move even a tenth of the earth necessary. There were countless landslides, owing to the practice of piling up the rubble on either side of the trenches as they went, and the torrential tropical rainstorms' effect upon same. Men were killed in mudslides and accidents, and a good deal of the work that had been done was undone by Mother Nature. The plan, for a channel with a uniform depth of 29.5 feet, a bottom width of 72 feet and a width at water level of 90 feet, meant that they had to move over 10 million cubic meters of earth, and they had not dealt with the natural bodies of water in the way.

Soon, another factor decimated the workforce: disease. Yellow fever began to spread throughout the camps. The French were plagued by biting insects called umbrella ants and set their bunk legs in bowls of water to discourage the pests from invading their beds. These proved to be marvelous breeding grounds for female *Stegomyia fasciata* mosquitoes, the carriers of yellow fever and malaria. In 1880, U.S. Navy Commander Thomas O. Selfridge, on that mission to map the Panamanian wilderness, described "mosquitoes so thick I have seen them put out a lighted candle with their burnt bodies." (The disease was not halted until after the Americans took over the project many years later, and Dr. Walter Reed sent his protégé, Colonel William C. Gorgas, to the site to wage a campaign against the insects.) There were tarantulas and scorpions, tropical spiders of truly horrendous size and coloration, biting flies and deadly snakes. Poor sanitation, including open toilet pits, claimed many more lives.

By 1888, it was clear that de Lesseps's project was a failure. The grandly named Compagnie was forced to declare bankruptcy. It had spent over $234 million, only a third of it spent on the construction itself, and killed over 20,000 men, without digging more than 40 percent of the way between the oceans it had been intended to unite. In 1889, the remaining assets of the company went into receivership. De Lesseps died in Paris in 1894. The Panama Canal was completed in 1914, with the financial support of the U.S. government and after some serious improvements in earth-moving technology.

You Put Him in Charge of What?

Politicians provide an endless supply of gaffes, mistakes, and blatant stupidity. Normally these annoy or even hurt those they represent. It is nice to see how some mistakes, even if they seemed a disaster to those making them, may have worked out quite well for the rest of the United States.

PRESIDENT MCKINLEY AND UNDERSECRETARY OF THE NAVY THEODORE ROOSEVELT

WASHINGTON, 1896

Paul A. Thomsen

By the 1890s, many thought the country had settled into its place as a contented democratic power, defined by a self-indulgent domestic bourgeois orientation, and a relatively minor political player on the world stage, but they had considered neither the rising expectations of the American working class nor their resourceful grassroots leadership.

With the decline of an active executive branch after the Civil War, the American corporate sector rapidly outgrew the shopkeeper and storefront to become heavy competition in the Industrial Age (a few successful examples include such familiar names as Sears, General Electric, Coca-Cola, and the Hearst newspapers). The growth of industry, however, also brought foul byproducts in the form of back-alley political deals, unsafe working conditions and widespread graft among the elite and influential. Almost overnight, corruption, once confined to the back rooms of inner-city political machines, gentlemen's clubs and legislative cloakrooms, ran rampant across the American political, economic and social landscape.

Attracted by the interest of the media investigating numerous allegations in self-serving pursuit of the sellable sensationalist copy, a few inner-city reformers and liberal thinkers joined with members of the Republican Party (including William McKinley, Carl Schurz, and Theodore Roosevelt) to upset their uncaring neighbors, unfair employers, and political competitors' illicit/immoral activities with a nonstop lobbying campaign and venture of investigative exposition. In time they merged with other political elements to form the Progressive Movement. They garnered modest successes in changing the new unbalanced status quo, winning key victories over political corruption and pressing for corrective legislation against the abuses of big business and inadequacies in the American welfare system, but the breakout Republicans had captured one thing more— national prominence.

Although McKinley came to serve as a key leader of peaceful and patriotic reformers, he was by no means an altruist. In embracing the growing interests of small businesses and the working class, the adventurous Republicans found new leverage against several key Democratic machine-run states (including New York's Tammany Hall machine). Flocking to the banner of their most electable candidate, William McKinley, the Republicans and their newfound allies and admirers successfully courted the general populace. As a result, they were victorious in 1896 over Democratic presidential challenger William Jennings Bryan.

As a former chairman of the House Ways and Means Committee and past electoral victim of the Democratic Party's rise to power, William McKinley knew the Republican victory might be short-lived if he failed to unify the country (which ironically meant alienating, if not entirely abandoning, his more liberal-minded reformer allies). Not long after the election, McKinley tried to engineer his forthcoming administration's future in the form of several anemic domestic and international policies. Deeply rooted in noninterventionism (a popular prospect with voters since the Washington presidency), domestically the president-elect compensated for this fledgling administration's apparent lack of drive by surrounding himself with famous and influential reformers, including former Lincoln secretary John Hay, federal circuit judge William H. Taft, and Massachusetts power broker and congressman Henry Cabot Lodge.

Still, McKinley's administration and advisors knew they lacked a certain connectivity with the working class, with the young Republicans, and with the key sector of every major presidential election, the city of New York. If the Republicans were to continue to occupy the political high ground, Taft, Lodge, and others knew they would need to bring forward a personal embodiment of these points and others. After careful consideration, they offered McKinley one name, Theodore Roosevelt.

The son of a semi-affluent New York family, in a few short years Theodore Roosevelt had become popularly recognized as a man of strong convictions and stalwart resolve who eagerly rose to the challenge of a changing world of rapid mechanization, expanding responsibilities, and arresting dangers. Embracing the philosophy of the "strenuous life (growth and strength through the conquest of adversity)," Roosevelt had overcome asthma, excelled as a rancher in the Dakota Territory, written several popular and academic volumes, served the Republican Party, and worked tirelessly as the police commissioner of the City of New York.

While Theodore Roosevelt had made many enemies in New York politics with his reformist victories, many saw him as the man to drag a muddled Washington bureaucracy and outmoded American military into the inner sanctum of the great Western powers. Though initially overlooked by McKinley, as Roosevelt was "always getting into rows with everybody," the president-elect warmed to the man and placed the former New York firebrand in a relatively insulated position in his administration as the non-decision-making assistant secretary of the navy. Roosevelt would, in essence, become a toothless dog, all bark and no bite. After all, they thought, what harm could he do if he was kept busy with running unending series of tedious administrative errands?

After a brisk summer of report readings, military consultation, and innocuous facility inspections, the new assistant secretary of the navy set about improving America's standing as a world power with his limited resources. As Roosevelt began overseeing weapons tests, personnel shifts, and supply reorganizations, he publicly shared his views of his administration. He called cowardice "an unpardonable sin," charged that "no national life is worth having if the nation is not willing, when the need shall arise, to stake everything on the supreme arbitrate of war, and to pour out its blood, its treasures, its tears like water rather than to admit to the loss of honor and renown," and charged the navy with overcoming tradition in the pursuit of war preparedness and eternal vigilance.

President McKinley and Secretary of Navy John Long scolded Theodore Roosevelt for his presumptuousness and inflammatory rhetoric but went no further. The assistant secretary of the navy's words, deemed the idiosyncratic trappings of an attention-grabbing upstart New Yorker, were considered brief flashes of annoyance when measured against the positive image Roosevelt held with the press as well as the general public. Even an angry toothless dog could be kept at heel if tethered to a short enough leash.

Meanwhile, the island of Cuba was in revolt.

Though a seemingly inconsequential geographic location, the Spanish-held Caribbean island had been a key trading point for centuries of American–European commerce, but as the Triangle Trade (slaves to sugar/molasses to rum) grew obsolete with the demise of the international slave trade and the rise of the machine age, the island's international importance and economic feasibility sharply declined (as did the failing power of the Spanish Empire). Long past their former glory, the once-grand European power of Spain and her minor Caribbean colony had been reduced to the level of subsistence at the price of her lower classes.

Ironically, in the last few decades of the nineteenth century, the United States had just about become Spanish Cuba's main economic investor (according to Stefan Lorant in *The Life and Times of Theodore Roosevelt*, in 1893 alone the United States had held $100 million in trade with the meager island nation), but American speculation in Cuba's sugar harvesting and related industries in recent years was becoming strained. Determined to wring their full measure from the colonials, Spain turned toward the employment of excessive military force to extract more economic worth from the already strained colony. Pushed too far, the Cuban people took to the hills and the streets in protest and the island devolved into revolution.

Though Spain had put down similar rebellions across their once-world-spanning empire in the past, the empire had never before met the outrage and indignation of the American press or the deft machinations of America's political undercurrent. Each day mainstream and yellow journalists across the United States fanned the flames of outrage and righteous indignation as they painted the colonies of the failing Spanish Empire in the same colors as America's first generation of revolutionaries. As Spain moved to implement extreme measures to pacify the rebellion, the American populace added their voice in support of "Cuba Libre," and Theodore Roosevelt made his move.

Throwing caution to the wind, Assistant Secretary Roosevelt and his kindred intellects emerged from the McKinley administration to press their point home before more conciliatory voices could interrupt this new infusion of forward momentum. Wielding the precepts of the Monroe Doctrine (asserting the position of the United States in all territorial matters surrounding her borders), the men called for military preparedness to put Spain out of the Western Hemisphere. Within the Department of the Navy Roosevelt, no longer characterized as a sensationalist or undue alarmist, likewise, openly pursued an active schedule of equipment and seaman preparedness, the implementation of state-of-the-art technology and rapid expansion of the American fleet.

President McKinley and Secretary Long, favoring a quiet diplomatic solution to the Cuban problem, were caught unprepared by the jingoistic tide supporting war with Spain. Though Roosevelt had been publicly silent on the issue for several months, others among the yellow press had taken up the conspirator's cause. Still, the administration held to the standard of benign acts of distant diplomacy and refused to publicly dignify the propaganda.

For several months the situation remained relatively stable. It seemed as if the entire situation might blow over, but in an unexpected and much-debated event, word reached the naval department that one of her ships, designated USS *Maine*, had exploded while at anchor in Havana Harbor.

With the apparent loss of hundreds of sailors, McKinley was sickened and Roosevelt found new hope. Enflamed by rhetoric critical of the quiet stance of the McKinley administration, the American public put their faith in the reported belief that a Spanish mine had detonated against the vessel's hull (recently disproven but still debated to this day) and cried for repayment with Spanish blood. The McKinley administration, however, viewed the entire journalistic endeavor as an absurd escapade undeserving of correction or commentary. The White House, viewing the *Maine* situation as a coincidental seaborne accident, looked upon the situation as diminishing further in international and national importance with each passing day.

Similarly, after the chiding of a few months prior and apparently sufficient quiet penance on behalf of his adjutant without a repeat incident, Secretary Long deemed Roosevelt's zeal sufficiently curtailed to mind the Department of the Navy for a single day while he took a much-needed rest. However, before partaking of a brief respite, on February 25, 1898, Long explicitly ordered Theodore Roosevelt not to do *anything* without first checking with either himself or the president. Having properly admonished his subordinate, the secretary of the navy promptly departed and eagerly embraced his well-deserved rest.

Acting Secretary Roosevelt made the most of his newfound temporary power and anxiously seized the opportunity presented him. First, he cabled the commander of the Asiatic Squadron, Commodore George Dewey, with orders to keep his vessels well stocked with fuel and provisions and, in the event of war, directed him to make best speed for the bulk of the Spanish fleet, moored in the Philippines, and send them to the bottom. Roosevelt then cabled similar Atlantic-based target instructions and rally points to Dewey's South Atlantic and European-based counterparts. Finally, the acting secretary also ordered the acquisition of as much coal as the United States could obtain from Far East markets, requisitioned the stockpiling of extra ammunition, the creation of guns from several naval yards, sent messages to Congress calling for the immediate authorization to enlist an unlimited number of seamen, and urged the New York adjutant general to commence planning for the transport of war supplies should hostilities soon erupt. Knowing the Spanish Empire and his journalistic admirers would be watching, Roosevelt calculated the brazen moves would add sufficient fuel to the fire and possibly provoke Spain into making the proper antagonistic move to validate the onset of war.

When the secretary of the navy returned the next morning fully refreshed and temporarily renewed, Secretary Long learned what his subordinate had done. He stated that in the space of a handful of hours Theodore Roosevelt had managed to "come very near causing more of an explosion than happened to the *Maine*." Long, at first apoplectic, began to try to reverse the damage, but the effects of Roosevelt's orchestration had already begun to destabilize the precarious diplomatic situation. Spain, having witnessed the ire of the American public and weighed down by the costly efforts of putting down the repeated armed rebellion in Cuba, began to reconsider its position. When Spain refused to grant Cuba independence—a stipulation the voting public insisted McKinley tender the apparently belligerent empire—the isolationist work of the old White House guard came undone.

By the end of April 1898 America's naval forces carried out the preponderance of Roosevelt's crafted war plan. Though Secretary Long would not authorize attacking the Spanish coast, Commodore Dewey carried out his orders to neutralize Spain's fleet at Manila, catching the enemy vessels at rest in the harbor and rendering them entirely unusable in a single night raid. McKinley had little choice but to give the American nation and Theodore Roosevelt the war they both wanted.

The McKinley administration reluctantly lauded Theodore Roosevelt for his handling and organization of the U.S. Navy. The short conflict, called the Spanish-American War, brought about several major advancements for a country whose leaders struggled to remain apart from the rest of the world. It revitalized the United States economy, liberated both Cuba and the Philippines from Spain and established several new benchmarks in military technology, training and strategy.

On a less tangible level, the political war machinations also brought about the realization of Theodore Roosevelt's desire to advance his country's prominence on the world stage and won President McKinley an unchallengeable vice-presidential running mate for his second administration. The president's pet turned out not to be a toothless dog but a war hound of the first order and, indeed, was McKinley's successor to the presidency.

You Hit What?

How can you have a book on massive mistakes without this one? You can't, so here it is . . .

CAPTAIN EDWARD J. SMITH
THE MID-ATLANTIC, 1912

Paul Kupperberg

She was the largest man-made object in the world, one of the wonders of her age. She was the last word in luxury and refinement, a blend of nineteenth-century Edwardian opulence and twentieth-century technology, the perfect representation of her time and place. She was the RMS *Titanic*, and, in retrospect, this grand lady of the sea seems to have been, as much as anything, a disaster waiting to happen.

The *Titanic* set off on her maiden voyage on April 10, 1912, from Southampton, England, in an era when the men and women listed on the Social Register were the celebrities and rock stars of the day. It was a time when the comings and goings of an upper class with names like Astor, Vanderbilt, and Straus were regularly reported in newspapers and one's standing in the social pecking order was judged by the extravagance of travel arrangements for voyages between Europe and the United States. The *Titanic*, the largest and most luxurious ship ever built, would sail with some of the most famous names of commerce, industry, and the arts filling her finely appointed cabins.

She was under the command of Captain Edward J. Smith, senior captain of the White Star Line and a celebrity in his own right with wealthy travelers. He was known as the Millionaire's Captain and had a long list of loyal clientele who cared less which ship they sailed on than that Smith was her captain. Sixty-two years old at the time he took the helm of the *Titanic,* the ship's first voyage was to be his last before retirement.

Beyond the high standards of luxury and Captain Smith's sterling reputation, the *Titanic* had gained fame with her reputation for being unsinkable. Constructed by the shipbuilding firm of Harland and Wolff of Belfast, Ireland, the sky was the limit for this mighty floating hotel. No expense was spared in her construction, from sumptuous appointments to safety features. The $7.5 million price tag (some $185 million in today's dollars) included a series of sixteen automatic watertight compartments, any three of which could flood without sinking the ship. For routine transatlantic crossings, even the most pessimistic shipbuilder could not have imagined a disaster capable of foundering the majestic liner.

Captain Smith himself was among those who believed the ship's publicity. The society captain freely expressed his confidence in the *Titanic* and her sister ship, the *Olympic.* He told friends, "Either of these vessels could be cut in halves and each half would remain afloat almost indefinitely. The non-sinkable vessel has been reached in these two wonderful craft."

On the surface, it seemed as though Captain Smith had ample reason to be sanguine. Born on January 27, 1850, in Hanley, Stoke-on-Trent of Staffordshire, he was married and had one child, and a career with White Star that began in 1880 as the fourth officer on the *Celtic.* He later commanded the *Majestic,* the *Adriatic, Celtic,*

Coptic, Germanic, Olympic, and several others. His reputation continued to grow. "When anyone asks me how I can best describe my forty years at sea," Captain Smith was widely reported as saying, "I merely say 'uneventful.' I have never been in an accident of any sort worth speaking about. I cannot imagine any condition which would cause a ship to founder. Modern ship building has gone beyond that."

Modern shipbuilding had reached its pinnacle with the *Titanic.* She was 882.5 feet long (compare that to a modern aircraft carrier at approximately 900 feet in length), 92.5 feet wide at the beam, and weighed in at 46,328 tons. The *Titanic* carried twenty-nine 100-ton boilers, which produced 55,000 horsepower to drive her two sets of four-cylinder reciprocating engines at speeds up to twenty-five knots.

She was the first ship to have a swimming pool. Her accommodations included First Class Staterooms available in any one of seven architectural styles, two first-class stairways (including a Grand Staircase of polished oak, decorated with a bronze cherub, a clock, and gold-plated light fixtures as well as natural light from a domed overhead skylight), a luxuriously wood-paneled and decorated First Class Lounge, a Smoking Room fitted with stained-glass windows, a hundred-foot-long Dining Salon, the Verandah Café, a Turkish bath, a squash court, a gymnasium, and four electric elevators. The *Titanic* was designed to carry as many as 2,599 passengers and 903 officers and crew.

The ship had been outfitted with sixteen sets of double-action boat davits, enough to hold forty-eight lifeboats, but she carried only fourteen regular lifeboats (seating 65 people each), two emergency sea boats (seating 35 each), as well as four smaller collapsible boats (seating 49 each). Filled to capacity, these boats could have carried 1,176 people to safety. There were life belts available for all, but they were of little help in surviving the freezing waters of the North Atlantic.

When the *Titanic* struck an iceberg some four hundred miles off the coast of Newfoundland on April 14, 1912, at 11:40 P.M., she was sailing with 2,223 passengers and crew. Of that number only 706 made it into lifeboats, many of which were lowered from the doomed liner with fewer than a third of their seats filled. The rest, 1,517 men, women, and children, went down with the great ship when it finally sank beneath calm waters at about 2:20 A.M. A more careful loading of the available boats could have saved over three hundred more people.

But no matter the number of seats filled, the *Titanic* and a majority of those she carried were doomed, because a seat on a lifeboat for every person on board was not required! Not by the British Board of Trade, which had authority over British shipping, nor by U.S. authorities with jurisdiction over ships entering American ports.

Captain Smith had admitted, while commanding the *Olympic*, that additional safety equipment was needed, but that White Star did not provide it, "not due to a desire . . . to save money, but rather because they believed their ships to be safe. Lifeboats were thought to be required . . . only in cases in which passengers were to be landed."

In spite of his stated concern, the captain was amazingly lax in matters of safety. The closest thing to a lifeboat drill held on the ship had been the brief lowering of two boats into the water on the starboard side while still docked at Southampton. A list of lifeboat stations for crew members wasn't posted until several days into the voyage, nor were passengers ever drilled in emergency procedures.

For all Smith's faith in his floating charge, the question arises of just how much faith should have been placed in the Millionaire's Captain by his employers. Despite his assertion of an "uneventful" life at sea, Smith's record was hardly spotless. While it's true he had been involved in only relatively minor accidents, they all seemed to point to the fact that the modern superliners had grown too large for Smith's knowledge and experience as a seaman.

In 1911, Captain Smith was given command of the *Olympic*, until *Titanic's* commissioning the largest ship afloat. She was almost twice as big as any ship he had ever handled, and his inexperience showed through on the ship's maiden voyage on June 21, 1911. As the giant liner was being moved into her slip, the tug the *O. L. Hallenbeck* was sucked against the *Olympic*, cutting off the smaller ship's stern frame, rudder, and wheel shaft after a sudden reverse burst of the giant ship's starboard rudder.

Several months later, on September 20, 1911, the *Olympic* collided with the Royal Navy cruiser *Hawke* in a narrow channel off the Isle of Wight.

Yet in spite of these incidents and in spite of this apparent proof that he was unaware of the displacement effects of a ship the size of the *Olympic*, he was allowed to continue commanding superliners, perhaps on the assumption that any captain could navigate any ship, regardless of her size.

It was such a miscalculation that caused the *Titanic's* famous encounter with an iceberg. In fact, even as the *Titanic* left her berth at Southampton on Wednesday, April 10, at 12:15 P.M., Captain Smith's awkwardness with this behemoth of a ship caused yet another, albeit minor, incident. The backwash from the *Titanic's* starboard propeller carried away the moorings of another liner, the *New York*. The *Titanic's* maiden voyage had to be delayed by half an hour until the smaller ship could be secured.

The rest of the voyage went off without a hitch. Though cold— the water temperature in the North Atlantic hovered around the freezing mark—the weather was uniformly clear, the sea calm. The *Titanic's* radio operator began receiving wireless warnings of ice in the area from nearby ships on Sunday, April 14. At least seven separate warnings were logged and reported to Captain Smith or his senior crew throughout the day, some of ice as near as five miles from the *Titanic's* position. But neither Smith nor his officers seemed overly concerned. Even in the face of the warnings, the captain ordered the ship to maintain her cruising speed of twenty-one knots. There are some who believe the captain was under pressure by J. Bruce Ismay, managing director of the White Star Line and a passenger on this voyage, to push the *Titanic* in order to beat the *Olympic's* old speed record for the Atlantic crossing. Not only was the *Titanic* the largest ship afloat, she was going to be the fastest as well.

Only about an hour before encountering the iceberg, the *Titanic* had received a wireless message from the steamship *Amerika*: "We are stopped and surrounded by ice." The radio operator of the *Titanic* couldn't be bothered, replying, "Shut up. I am busy. I am working [i.e., sending passenger messages to] Cape Race [Newfoundland]."

In spite of these warnings, Captain Smith did almost nothing. He took no precautions other than to warn the posted lookouts to keep "a sharp lookout for ice."

He did not increase the watch.

He did not slow the ship.

Captain Smith merely pocketed the wireless warnings, then turned the helm over to his first officer and retired to attend a dinner being given in his honor.

Any one of these precautions could have saved the *Titanic*, perhaps not from the collision itself but almost certainly from the catastrophe that followed. Additional men on watch might have spotted the iceberg sooner, giving the massive ship time to stop or turn. Likewise, had the *Titanic* been traveling at a slower speed, she would have had the time to steer around the massive mountain of ice. As it was—and as was learned more than seventy years later, when the wreck of the *Titanic* was finally located 12,000 feet below the surface and the damage could at long last be examined—the ship might have even survived the collision had the well-intended first officer not ordered the ship turned "hard astarboard." The bow began to swing to port at the last second, her starboard side scraping hard against the massive iceberg, popping bolts that held the steel plates of the hull together. The damage stretched along three hundred feet of hull, across six of the watertight compartments, twenty feet below the waterline, allowing water to flood into the ship.

It's now believed that had the *Titanic* struck the iceberg head-on she would have sustained damage to the first two or three watertight compartments, but she most certainly would have remained afloat. In all likelihood, she would even have been able to make it to port in Newfoundland under her own steam.

But the Millionaire's Captain, the senior man of the White Star fleet, did not take into account the momentum of a 46,328-ton object moving at twenty-one or twenty-two knots through the water. He did not seem to give any thought to what was required to bring such a behemoth to a full stop under emergency conditions. It took more than forty seconds for the *Titanic* to even begin to respond and start its starboard turn away from the ice.

In the end, hearings into the cause of the disaster were held in both the United States and Great Britain. The two inquiries came to essentially the same conclusions and offered much the same recommendations. They called for lifeboat space enough for every person on all foreign and domestic ships entering their ports, mandatory lifeboat drills, improved ship designs, and the twenty-four-hour operation of radiotelegraph equipment.

The White Star Line took its share of the blame for this tragic loss of life. In summary, Senator William Alden Smith said the *Titanic*'s builders were "so confident . . . no life-saving or signal devices were reviewed . . . no drill or station practice or helpful discipline disturbed the tranquility of that voyage, and when the crisis came a state of absolute unpreparedness stupefied both passengers and crew, and in their despair the ship went down. . . ."

Nor did Captain Smith escape condemnation, gently though it was worded in the U.S. Senate Inquiry's final report: "Captain Smith knew the sea and his clear eye and steady hand had often guided his ship through dangerous paths. For 40 years storms sought in vain to vex him or menace his craft. . . . Each new advancing type of ship built by his company was handed over to him as a reward for faithful services and as an evidence of confidence in his skill. Strong of limb, intent of purpose, pure in character, dauntless as a sailor should be, he walked the deck of his majestic structure as master of her keel.

"Titanic though she was," Senator Smith continued, "[Smith's] indifference to danger was one of the direct and contributing causes of this unnecessary tragedy . . . overconfidence seems to have dulled the faculties usually so alert. With the atmosphere literally charged with warning signals and wireless messages registering their last appeal, the stokers in the engine room fed their fires with fresh fuel, registering in that dangerous place her fastest speed."

And for want of another set of eyes on watch for obstacles in her path or the commonsense command to slow down in dangerous waters, the greatest maritime disaster in history sent 1,517 souls to their death.

In the end, however, Edward Smith did what any good captain would. He went down with his ship.

You Demand What?

Sometimes even the most gifted author is a lot dumber than the characters he creates. See what we mean with this romp through literary stupidity.

AUTHORS, EVERYWHERE, ALL THE TIME

Brian M. Thomsen

No one ever said that authors were perfect.

Far from it.

Margaret Mitchell thought Groucho Marx would be the perfect thespian to assay the role of Rhett Butler in *Gone With the Wind*.

John Kennedy O'Toole killed himself when he had trouble placing *A Confederacy of Dunces* at the publishing house of his choice.

And it is even rumored that an author turned down having his novel chosen as an Oprah pick.

Some authors even took action to derail themselves from the gravy train that their ongoing works had provided for them.

Sir Arthur Conan Doyle had a quiet medical practice in Southsea, England, where he dabbled in storytelling in his off hours, occasionally making a sale to one of the literary magazines such as the *Strand*. One of these stories, a novelette entitled "A Study in Scarlet," introduced the now-famous consulting detective Sherlock

Holmes to the world. Unfortunately, Doyle soon tired of his creation and after twenty-four stories and another novelette by the name of "The Sign of Four" decided to remove himself from the successful series that he felt was getting in the way of his other works.

So in a story entitled "The Final Problem" Holmes finally confronts his archnemesis and, in a life-and-death struggle, falls with him to both of their deaths over a waterfall.

The *Strand* was disappointed at the prospect of no new Holmes stories, and readers were devastated.

Though Doyle continued to be published, his literary fame and following began to dissipate as it soon became apparent that there were more Holmes fans than Doyle fans. As a result, ten years later Doyle resurrected his detective in a series of new stories that started off with what really happened at the end of "The Final Problem," whereby Holmes managed to survive . . . as did the literary career of Doyle.

A similar situation existed with retired spy Ian Fleming, whose creation of secret agent MI5 hero James Bond provided him with a nice supplement to his pension from the Crown.

After the initial surprise success of *Casino Royale* (1953), Fleming found himself pressured to continue the series with a new book each year. The 1954 book *Live and Let Die* did fine and met with Fleming's own satisfaction, but subsequent volumes (*Moonraker* and *Diamonds Are Forever*) were not as strong, and definitely showed signs of a waning of interest on the part of the author despite the ongoing commercial success of the series, and as long as the books sold the publishers wanted more.

Fleming saw only one way out of his gilded cage, so in the next book in the series, *From Russia with Love,* he conspired against his hero and delivered probably the best Bond book of all time, with one unfortunate problem: Bond died on the last page of the book.

The publisher wasn't pleased, and the readers were shocked, but what Fleming had done, he had done, and there was no turning back.

Or was there?

In his administering of his coup de grâce for James Bond, Fleming became reinterested in his character and began to think of ways of making the series more interesting for himself, so much so that he even regretted killing the master spy.

So what did he do?

He admitted his mistake to his publisher and resurrected the resilient spy in a new book in the series the following year, and though the explanation of his survival was lame and contrived, no one cared.

Bond was back and better than ever.

Sometimes mortal mistakes are not forever, and indeed some characters do only live twice.

Author mistakes aren't always confined to their fictional works either.

Sometimes, in hindsight, they screw up on the business side.

Sometimes it's a binding option clause that ties up not just the current book but all future works as well, or a term of contract clause that wraps the work up for infinity with language such as "as long as the book remains in print the contract shall remain in force at its original terms," thus precluding any future renegotiation in the event of unexpected and extreme success.

Sometimes the writer finds himself subservient to another individual who controls the actual content of a work. This is most prevalent in nonfiction where a celebrity or authority can sell a book without actually writing it. The story and authority are theirs, but it is up to a real writer to put it on the printed page, whether working from notes, research or interviews with the subject at hand. In such cases the writer in question is usually paid more upfront for his services than he would get on a book of his own, but his or her participation in future profits would be more limited or in some cases not at all.

Such is the case of William Novak, who was the author of the number-one nonfiction bestseller of 1984/1985. It was called *Iacocca: An Autobiography,* for which Novak received second billing under Iacocca, and an up-front flat fee with no participation in any future revenues or royalties.

I'm sure at the time he handed the book in, Novak felt well compensated.

I am equally sure that he felt less so after the book had sold its first one million copies.

You Ignored Whose Warning?

On September 11, 2001, terrorists rammed their stolen jetliners into the World Trade Center, killing 3,000 people and changing the world forever. But compared to another much more destructive force, their efforts pale.

GALVESTON, TEXAS, 1900

Mike Resnick

Let's turn the clock back 101 years and 3 days, and move the locale from Manhattan to Galveston, Texas.

The United States government had a relatively new agency: the U.S. Weather Bureau. The same one you get on your cable TV, or that your local newscast quotes when telling you to wear your raincoat or your galoshes. *That* weather bureau.

It was a new science, forecasting the weather. Oh, people had been *predicting* the weather for centuries. See a hairy caterpillar in October? Bad winter coming. Did the June bugs show up in late April? Long, dry summer on tap. You know the routine.

But then, in 1900, weather forecasting was finally recognized as a science. They used instruments. They studied the barometric reading. They contacted outposts in all directions to track storms. They were the newest of the new, these weather forecasters.

And they protected their turf.

We'll get back to them in a minute, but first let me tell you a little bit about Galveston, because these days it's dwarfed in its own home state by Dallas and Houston and San Antonio—but back then, in 1900, it ranked behind only Houston as the major city of Texas. Not only that, but in the entire country it was second only to New York City as an entry point for immigrants. In fact, it was nicknamed the "Western Ellis Island."

How big was it? Well, the population was always in flux due to immigration, but the best estimate was 30,000, give or take. The climate was pleasant, the land was lovely, property was inexpensive, and though it was on the water everyone knew it was safe from typhoons and hurricanes and the like. And if they didn't know, the Weather Bureau was only too happy to tell them so.

The shining light of the Galveston Weather Bureau was a gentleman named Isaac Cline. He was their superstar. Cline was quoted as saying that it was "an absurd delusion" for anyone to think Galveston could possibly ever suffer serious damage from a hurricane.

He based this conclusion on two erroneous beliefs: first, that any high surf or storm tide would flow over Galveston into the bay behind it and then into the Texas prairie, doing no lasting damage at all; and second, because of the shallow slope of the Gulf coastline, the incoming surf would be broken up and made much less dangerous.

Cline was so sure of this that he ridiculed the notion of building a seawall to withstand storms, and because he was, for all practical purposes, the voice of the U.S. government on this particular subject, the wall was never built.

Now, the Weather Bureau was still in its infancy, but the people manning the Galveston division were pretty confident in their skills. Certainly more confident than they were of the skills of the

Cubans they had defeated just two years earlier when Teddy Roosevelt led his Rough Riders up San Juan Hill. The Cuban weathermen *meant* well, decided the Galveston Weather Bureau, but after all, they were just illiterate peasants, right?

So when, on September 7, 1900, Cuba began reporting that the biggest storm anyone had ever seen was heading right toward Galveston, the Weather Bureau was so sure they were totally mistaken and panicking needlessly that they refused to make the Cubans' warnings public.

After all, everyone *knew* that Galveston couldn't suffer serious damage from a storm. Either it would turn away before reaching shore, or it would pass right over and blow itself out somewhere over the vast Texas prairie.

But by the morning of September 8, it became apparent to Cline and his coworkers that the storm *wasn't* going to turn away and miss Galveston. In fact, it was apparent to everyone in the city. All they had to do was look to the south and east and see what was approaching.

Should they evacuate the city? they wanted to know.

Certainly not, Cline and the Weather Bureau assured them. This is Galveston, not some shantytown that's likely to get blown away by a strong wind. Our houses are well built, we're sitting right on the slope of the Gulf coastline, and haven't you ever seen a thunderstorm before?

So the people—most of them, anyway—trusted their government bureaucrats and stayed put.

At least until the water became knee-high, and then waist-high, and then neck-high. Pretty soon those who hadn't fled the town were perched on their roofs.

And pretty soon after that there weren't any roofs, because the houses began collapsing, and boats capsized, and bodies—infants and the elderly at first, then men and women in their primes—began floating down the streets, through the windows, over the vanished roofs.

And still the storm continued.

At one point a train from Beaumont entered the town but halted well short of the station. The passengers wanted to leave and find some high ground, or at least some rooftops, for safety. The conductors, hearing the reassurances of the Weather Bureau, urged the passengers to remain where they were. After all, this was a *train,* a massive thing of steel. Surely no storm can harm it or wash it away, and you don't have to take *our* word for it; just ask the Weather Bureau.

Ten passengers looked out the window, said, in essence, "Bullshit!," and waded and swam through the rampaging water to try to find some safe haven. Eighty-five passengers believed the bureaucrats of the Weather Bureau and stayed with the train.

By the next morning, all eighty-five were dead.

I should add that this wasn't entirely the fault of Cline and his Galveston bureaucrats. They were in contact with a branch of the bureau in the West Indies, which was anxious to show up the Cubans—their recent enemies—and to prove that these Spanish peons were pressing the panic button needlessly.

Of course, back in Galveston, by the time it became clear that, if anything, the Cubans were *underestimating* the danger, no one could find the panic button. It was hidden under tons of water.

So did help rush in, as Americans have always helped their own and others?

Nope.

You see, Cline was in control of the forecasting, but his immediate superior, Willis Moore, was in control of the whole damned Galveston Bureau, and Moore was more concerned with Galveston's—and his bureau's—image than with saving citizens that he had convinced himself weren't really in all that much danger to begin with. So a call for help never went out.

The city's newspapers colluded with the bureau, and downplayed the story. In fact, an unpublished editorial in the *Galveston Tribune* the morning after the storm hit assured the public that there was very little danger from the storm, and "no possibility of serious loss of life."

Why (I hear you ask) was it unpublished?

Because the press floated out to sea before the issue could be printed.

All the phone and telegraph wires were dead by 4:00 P.M., and Galveston was effectively cut off from the rest of the world. By 7:00 P.M. the winds were over 120 miles an hour, and some were as high as 200 miles an hour before midnight. Contact wasn't reestablished with Galveston for another 28 hours, at 11:30 P.M. on September 9. In the interim, the closest any train had been able to approach the city was SIX miles. Anything beyond that was too dangerous.

When it was over, it was estimated that Galveston had lost between 3,000 and 4,000 houses and buildings.

It was always going to lose them. The people were something else again. If the bureaucrats of the Weather Bureau had simply told the truth, had shared the information they'd been sent from Cuba, had not been so pigheaded in their certainty that no storm could ever damage Galveston . . .

No one knows exactly how many people died in New York on September 11, 2001. The best estimate is 3,000, out of a population of more than seven million. That comes to four ten-thousandths of one percent.

No one knows exactly how many people died in Galveston on September 8 and 9, 1900. The best estimate is 10,000, out of a population of about 30,000. That comes to 33 percent.

It should be obvious at this point that the destructive force greater than any terrorist's bomb was an arrogant bureaucracy, not the hurricane. Which is rather a pity as we can at least predict the course of hurricanes.

YOU UNLEASHED WHAT?

"Never start something you can't finish" is an old proverb. A pity that those who think their power is unlimited forget it so often. The Boxer Rebellion took place during the summer of 1900. By the time the conflict was over tens of thousands of people lay dead. The uprising led to the end of the Manchu dynasty and had such a negative impact on the Chinese psyche that it still colors that country's attitude toward the rest of the world.

TZU HSI, EMPRESS DOWAGER OF CHINA

CHINA, 1900

William C. Dietz

Who screwed up? The answer is Tzu Hsi, the sixty-five-year-old Empress Dowager of China, also known to her subjects as the Old Buddha. When the Boxer Rebellion began, Tzu Hsi had ruled one way or another for nearly half a century. Things had not gone well for the Chinese, starting with their loss of the Opium War in 1840–1842 and continuing with a long list of humiliating concessions as the great powers robbed China of Hong Kong, Manchuria, Burma, what is now Vietnam, and ended their longtime domination of Korea. Germany, Russia, France, Britain, Japan and the United States all took turns carving profitable slices off the once-great empire.

That's why Tzu Hsi hated the foreigners almost as much as the

Boxers did and sought to use the Boxers as the means not only to cleanse China of foreign influence but to preserve the Manchu dynasty. *It was a terrible mistake.*

The Boxers were a little-known, poorly organized cult that was born of two earlier groups, the Big Swords, which was a group of landlords, farmers and peasants organized to protect themselves from bandits, and the Spirit Boxers, who drew their members from the poorest of the poor, and routinely practiced martial arts in public places. Hence the name Boxers. During their demonstrations members would call upon well-known spirits to enter their bodies and participate in scenes of mass possession. The displays, which incorporated traditional folktales, drew large enthusiastic crowds.

Much like the French underground in World War II, or the shadowy terrorist organizations of today, the movement referred to as the Boxers was actually an amalgamation of smaller groups having no central leadership. Religion, in the form of the traditional gods that practitioners allowed to possess them, plus the Chinese folk operas that they borrowed for use in their demonstrations, allowed the Boxers to tap into a common vocabulary of deities, superstitions and fears.

As a result, the Boxers were able to convince many members of the populace that their rites rendered them invulnerable to bullets and other weapons—claims that adherents sought to prove during wild demonstrations, when members of the audience were challenged to attack them. The wounds they sometimes suffered were dismissed as a failure to use the correct techniques and had little or no effect on recruiting.

The movement spread quickly and became especially popular

in Shantung province, the place where Confucius was born. During the late 1800s not only was the area devastated by a series of natural disasters, including floods and plagues of locusts, it also came under attack from foreign technology, culture and religion.

Steamboats, trains and imported textiles put thousands out of work even as Christian missionaries roamed the land, built churches using funds extorted from the Chinese government and sought to turn the populace against their traditional gods.

No wonder then that it was in Shantung where the first missionaries were murdered and where the Boxers launched their initial attacks on thousands of Christian converts. Some were hacked to death, while others were skinned or buried alive.

Shortly thereafter, and with the assistance of the imperial troops that the empress supplied, the Boxers surrounded more than four thousand Chinese and foreigners in the port city of Tientsin, even as almost nine hundred citizens of eighteen foreign nations were trapped in the diplomatic quarter of Peking (now called Beijing).

Having been established during the years following Great Britain and France's defeat of China earlier in the century, the quarter was a bustling mix of foreign embassies, offices and stores where all manner of luxuries could be bought.

The ensuing siege lasted for two months and took place during the worst heat of the summer as thousands of Boxers and imperial troops tried in vain to take the diplomatic quarter. They attacked in waves, tunneled in under the walls, and burned a neighboring library filled with ancient texts in an effort to break through.

In the meantime American, British, French, Italian, Spanish, Russian, German and Japanese soldiers, diplomats, missionaries, journalists, socialites and adventurers of every stripe fought side by side to repel the oncoming hordes even as cowards hid in cellars, women made sandbags out of silk, and the warm humid air grew thick with the stink of rotting flesh. Food soon ran short, and denied an equitable distribution of what remained to be eaten, more than three thousand Chinese converts began to starve.

Finally, by the time foreign troops came to the rescue in August, more than two hundred of the foreigners holed up in Peking had been killed or wounded, an equal number of priests, nuns and missionaries had been murdered in the countryside, and tens of thousands of Chinese converts had been indiscriminately slaughtered. There is no way to know how many Boxers and imperials were killed—but it seems safe to say that the number was in the thousands.

Unfortunately the rebellion brought *more* foreigners into China; they cut the country into even smaller slices, and Tzu Hsi was eventually forced not only to enact the reforms that she hoped to avoid but to do so with such speed that they undercut the dynasty she sought to perpetuate. The Old Buddha died in 1908 and the last emperor was deposed three years later. Now, after some ninety-five years, we're left to ask "Manchu who?"

You Allowed What?

Here is a less than glowing . . . well, maybe glowing is too accurate a word . . . story of politics and a just plain lack of good sense. Or maybe someone forgot to tell him that Australia wasn't a penal colony anymore.

MARALINGA: AUSTRALIA'S NUCLEAR FOLLY

PRIME MINISTER CLEMENT ATLEE

AUSTRALIA, 1950

James A. Hartley

In 1950, Britain, hoping to proceed with its atomic weapon testing program, was denied use of the Nevada testing facilities in the United States. As a result, Labor prime minister Clement Atlee sent a top secret personal message to Australian prime minister Robert Menzies, a staunch Anglophile, asking if the Australian government might agree to the testing of British nuclear weapons at the Monte Bello Islands, off western Australia. In effect, Atlee asked Menzies if he could lend him his country for atomic tests. Menzies agreed immediately, with no record of him having consulted any of his cabinet colleagues on the matter. Menzies is known to have ruled his cabinet with an iron fist and is unlikely to have received much resistance anyway. The agreement was the start of a program of testing and involvement of the Australian people that was to last years, with little proper safeguards for the land or the people involved, even to the use of over 15,000 Australian servicemen to be involved in "safety testing," not to mention the Aboriginal population of the area.

Despite Atlee having mentioned the risk of radiation hazards in the initial tests, Menzies was happy to agree to the use of the site, only too pleased to assist the "motherland." It wasn't as if they didn't know at least some of the risks. The world had already seen Hiroshima and Nagasaki, and yet Menzies agreed without a question. Was it that he had his eventual knighthood in mind? Despite sending a telegram to Atlee after the initial Monte Bello tests, asking, "What the bloody hell is going on? The cloud is drifting over the mainland," Menzies went on to agree immediately to further tests on the Australian mainland proper, replying to Churchill promptly. These tests were to be held at Emu Field, northwest of Adelaide.

On October 15 1953, Totem I, a device of ten kilotons, was detonated, and two days later, Totem II at eight kilotons. Three days after the Totem trials, Australia was formally notified by the British government of its desire to create a nuclear test facility. In August 1954, the Australian cabinet agreed to the establishment of a permanent testing ground at a site that became named Maralinga, north of the transcontinental railway line in south Australia. Prime Minister Menzies was instrumental in pushing this agreement through.

In addition to the larger tests held at these sites, the British conducted over six hundred smaller trials, resulting in some 830 tons of debris contaminated by around twenty kilograms of plutonium, merely buried in twenty-one pits around the area. In addition, around two kilograms of plutonium was dispersed across the south Australian landscape during dispersal and fallout pattern trials held at the same time. By the time the British had finished their tests in 1958, twelve nuclear bombs had been exploded in the atmosphere about south and western Australia, and the minor tests had scattered millions of contaminated metal fragments almost one hundred miles from the test site at Maralinga. One area, covered with fine plutonium dust, will be uninhabitable for 240,000 years. The Australian Radiation Laboratory currently says that only "intermittent forays" of less than nine hours should be permitted in these areas.

Throughout the program, Britain kept the details of these tests secret, despite using Australia's land and people—secret even from the Australian government itself. Australia's compliance, spearheaded by Menzies, went much further than simply allowing the tests. In 2001, the British government admitted to using Australian servicemen in what it calls "clothing trials" after the Maralinga nuclear blasts in 1956. These servicemen were used in various exercises, one day after the explosions at ground zero, exercises that involved running, jumping and crawling over the landscape. According to the British Department of Defence, the purpose of these tests was to see if the uniforms were adequate. They weren't testing the people; they were testing the clothes. The people involved in these tests were called indoctrinees. Yet a year after those trials, protective clothing was still not available. According to Retired Major Alan Batchelor, when the explosions went off, they were positioned eight miles away, and then about an hour after, they had to go in and open up instrument shelters about a hundred yards away from ground zero, not wearing anything but working dress, rubber boots and cotton gloves. Even the slowest individual had to know some of the risks involved, and yet Menzies and his cabinet blithely agreed to use Australian servicemen as guinea pigs. It wasn't enough that they were making large areas of the continent unusable—they had to use people as well. What was wrong with British servicemen?

The whole affair goes further. According to records, security at the test sites was lax—the range boundaries were not properly monitored, allowing people to walk in and out. In one incident, in May 1957, four Aboriginal people were found camping in one of the bomb craters, not surprising considering that any warning signs posted were only in English, unintelligible to the local Aboriginals. This was yet another great idea put together by the government. There may be a local indigenous population, they may not be able to read, they may not be able to speak English, but we'll put up a few signs in English telling them to stay out. When authorities discovered them, the family was immediately taken to a decontamination center at the site and was required to shower. They were then driven away from the area. Any witness to the event was sworn to secrecy under the Official Secrets Act. This only came out later at a Royal Commission into the events, where a number of the documents had become declassified.

There is little doubt that the secrecy surrounding the program served British rather than Australian interests. Full disclosure of the hazards and potential cost was out of the question. The British even concealed the fact of the use of plutonium in the minor trials. Prime Minister Menzies had already been informed of several of the risks, yet he identified so strongly with Britain that he considered British national interests equivalent to Australia's, or maybe it was that he thought the Old Country would give him the honors he deserved. It wasn't quite enough to be leader of a hick nation that clearly didn't have a clue. On the few occasions when Australian authorities chose to assert themselves, it was purely symbolic. For example, the Australians objected to the name Volcano, as that probably just sounded too violent or explosive, and one of the series was renamed Antler. In another instance, a detonation scheduled for Sunday was postponed in deference to the Australian sensibilities.

Australia's compliance was further illustrated by the role of Sir Ernest Titterton. A British physicist, Titterton had worked on the Manhattan Project. In 1950, he was appointed chair of nuclear physics at the Australian National University. One of his first tasks in this role was advisor to the British scientific team at the first Monte Bello tests. In 1956, Australia established the Atomic Weapons Tests Safety Committee, responsible for monitoring the British tests. Titterton was a foundation member of the committee, and finally its chairman. While Menzies, on paper, had conceived of the committee as an independent, objective body, it is apparent that it was more sensitive to the needs of the British testing program that those of the Australian populace. Titterton is quoted as having said to the Royal Commission that if the Aboriginal people objected to the tests, they could have voted the government out, regardless of the fact that the Aboriginal people were denied full voting rights at the time of the tests, and were even excluded from the census until 1967.

The Australian government went out of its way to limit public knowledge and to shut down criticism, and there is little doubt that Menzies was at the head of these efforts. One patrol officer who objected that the development of testing sites was proceeding without proper attention to the local Aborigines was reminded of "his obligations as a Commonwealth Officer" and warned against speaking to the press. Another officer who reported sighting Aborigines in the prohibited zone was asked if he realized "what sort of damage he would be doing by finding Aboriginals where Aboriginals could not be." Australian journalists were also prohibited from publishing material relating to the tests unless it was celebratory.

After the final tests in 1957, the folly of the Australian government continued. In 1966, after a series of radiological tests, Britain mounted Operation Brumby to clean up the test area. During the operation, the twenty-one pits were filled with contaminated equipment and were capped with 650 tons of concrete. Instead of removing more of the radiated material, Britain merely plowed topsoil under to reduce surface contamination, making it harder to remove the material at all. A top-secret report on the operation was prepared, submitted to the Australian government, filed and promptly forgotten. Australian authorities subsequently signed documents absolving the British government from any further responsibility for the test sites, one in 1968 and another in 1979, after the removal of one pound of solid plutonium to Britain.

In 1984, when 3,000 square kilometers of land surrounding the test sites was due to be returned to the Tjurutja Aboriginal people, scientists of the Australian Radiation Laboratory carried out a radiological survey of the site. They were stunned to find that the levels of radioactivity were on the order of ten times higher than those reported by the British eight years earlier. They found significant contamination extending far beyond the fenced boundary. They concluded that as much as twenty kilograms of plutonium was distributed over the test area, not the two kilograms claimed by the British.

In response to the ARL findings, in July 1984 the Australian government set up the Royal Commission to inquire into British nuclear tests. The findings of the commission blamed Prime Minister Robert Menzies for the tests being held in Australia. It also found the British government to be guilty of concealing vital information on the tests from the Australian government and that, in collusion with nuclear scientist Professor Ernest Titterton, they had deliberately distorted facts. The commission also recommended that compensation for injuries sustained during and after the tests should be extended to Aborigines, particularly those exposed to the black mist that swept over them after some of the atomic tests.

Whether ill-informed, simply naïve, or prompted by a misguided loyalty to British interests, the Australian government of the time, under the iron leadership of Robert Menzies, Australia's longest serving prime minister, had embarked on a program that would do lasting damage to the Australian landscape and its people. Menzies was knighted in 1963 and retired only three years later in 1966. The cancer and radiation remain to this day.

You Are Doing It When, How?

Africa is a big continent, so big that we can't confine this section to a single story or example. It is just a too rich an assortment to not let you have a good selection of the amazing mistakes and wonderful absurdities that can be found on the Dark Continent.

Inefficiency is nothing new to Africa. That said, the fact remains that the governments of sub-Saharan Africa are constantly finding new and better ways to be inefficient. If nothing else, this is darkly humorous, unless you have to live with it, that is.

INEFFICIENCIES ON THE DARK CONTINENT;

OR, DARWIN WAS WRONG

AFRICA

Mike Resnick and Ralph Roberts

You Lost Our Navy?

SWAZILAND 2002

The most recent incident occurred in the fall of 2002, when an African nation lost its navy. Okay, it was a navy of just one ship, but still. . . .

"The situation is absolutely under control," Transport Minister Ephraem Magagula assured the Swaziland parliament in Mbabane, according to the *Johannesburg Star*. "Our nation's navy is perfectly safe. We just don't know where it is, that's all."

The navy in question was the landlocked country's only ship, the *Swazimar*. That's right— a navy of one ship. (Well, let's be rea-

sonable. Just how many naval vessels does a tiny landlocked country need anyway?)

Explained Magagula: "We believe it is at sea somewhere. We did
send a team of men to look for it, but there was a problem with
drink and they failed to find it, and so, technically, yes, it's temporarily lost. But I categorically reject all suggestions of incompe-
tence on the part of this government. The *Swazimar* is a big ship
painted in the sort of nice bright colors you can see at night. Mark
my words, it will turn up. The right honorable gentleman opposite
is a very naughty man, and he will laugh on the other side of his
face when my ship comes in."

When last we heard, Swaziland was still looking for its navy.

You Have How Many Wives?

SWAZILAND 2001

While we're on the subject of Swaziland, let us consider young
King Mswati II—one of the few absolute monarchs left anywhere
in the world.

King Mswati is the marrying kind. He recently took his tenth
wife, a seventeen-year-old schoolgirl. Of course, Mswati has quite
a way to go to match his daddy, old King Sobhuza II who died in
1986. Sobhuza had sixty wives and made sure he could keep them
by abolishing the constitution and all representative forms of government in Swaziland.

Mswati realized that marrying so many women in this day and
age might not sit well with his subjects, so he issued a degree that
gave him total censorship over all the media in his country, on the
not-unreasonable assumption that you can't get mad if you don't
know what's going on.

Then, since he had so many wives to transport on state visits to the far reaches of his country (which happens to be considerably smaller than Florida), Mswati contracted to buy a $50 million private jet while his nation of a million people is short on food and living on a per capita average of less than a dollar a day.

Or, as Mel Brooks says, "It's good to be the king!"

(And it's getting better. He just got engaged again.)

So how does the Studmuffin of Swaziland stack up against some of the recent African heads of state?

You Put the Money Where?

KENYA, 1977–PRESENT

Well, the champ is the late Joseph Mobutu (who changed his name to Mobutu Sese Seku), dictator (in Africa the term is "president-for-life") of Zaire. Mobuto came to power at the height of the Cold War, put his loyalty up for auction, and was purchased by the West. Over the years the United States and its allies gave Zaire $10 billion in aid. At the time of his death, Mobutu's Swiss bank accounts and European real estate holdings were estimated to be worth more than $9 billion.

Another African leader who won't be going hungry soon is Daniel Arap Moi, president of Kenya from 1978 until 2003. He'd been a schoolteacher before Jomo Kenyatta tapped him as his vice president, and he succeeded to the presidency shortly thereafter. With no savings, and on the minimal salary paid to Kenya's president, Moi managed to acquire the ownership of every gas station of a certain U.S./European petroleum company in Kenya (renamed Kobil gas stations), every Mercedes taxi in Nairobi and Mombasa, the entire Air Kenya fleet of DC-3 airplanes, and a few hundred thousand acres of prime farmland in Kenya's White Highlands. The only conclusion: he must have brown-bagged a *lot* of lunches.

But never let it be said that every African dictator takes it all with him. When the emperor Bokassa was being deposed in the Central African Republic, a mere handful of years after the French donated some $25 million to his Ascendancy Ceremony, one of his last imperial acts was to stop by the nation's treasury and set it afire.

You Set Up What on an Island?

IDI AMIN, UGANDA, 1969

Investing in African Real Estate

King Mswati uses his absolute rule for self-indulgence. Nothing unusual about that; being the top dog has always been a great way to get girls . . . literally, in his case.

But Uganda's Idi Amin, who just died in exile in Saudi Arabia, was a cat of a different stripe.

Being a total dictator, self-indulgent, and evil to boot, can start to wear on the old nerves. You need a holiday retreat of some sort. Old Idi had his—twenty-three-acre Mukusu Island on beautiful Lake Victoria. There Idi whiled away many a pleasant afternoon indulging in his hobby of torturing a wide variety of victims and feeding them to the crocodiles.

Today, over twenty years after the end of Idi Amin's genocidal dictatorship, this island still bears the scars of his lazy afternoons there. You might stop by it sometime: a great little fixer-upper, with cattle prods, chains, and crocodiles included. (Idi called it Paradise Island—perhaps because of the many people he and the crocs dispatched to Paradise while he was there.)

Amin had some other little problems in the area of civilized behavior. It's said on good authority that he ate at least one of his infant sons. He declared that Adolf Hitler was his hero and erected a statue of him in the capital city of Kampala. Math was never his strong suit, and he simply never understood why he couldn't just print more money when he needed it. So print it he did—and there came a day when a loaf of bread cost in excess of a million Ugandan shillings.

He remained convinced (deluded is probably a more accurate word) that his people wanted him back, and he left his Saudi reservation a few years ago, certain they were ready to roll out a red, if not bloodstained, carpet for him. He got as far as the Zaire-Uganda border when he was recognized and refused entry.

You Killed All the What?

REPUBLIC OF THE CONGO, 1960S

There were problems even before Idi Amin. . . .

Ruling Uganda stupidly didn't begin with Idi Amin, who took over in 1969. A few years earlier, the country was having a problem with tsetse flies.

Now, the tsetse fly tends to live on herbivores, usually wild ones—but if you bring enough cattle into an area, the tsetse isn't all that selective and will just as happily live, breed and dine on domestic cattle. The problem is, wild game has a built-in immunity to the tsetse fly, and domestic animals don't.

Now, in any reasonable society, if your cattle were infested with tsetse flies, you'd spray heavily with DDT or something similar, and of course you'd begin dipping your livestock regularly.

But this was Uganda. Let us, they reasoned, get rid of the wildlife, and then the tsetse flies will have nowhere to go.

So they declared an unlimited open season on their game. Hunters came from all over. It's estimated that half a million animals were killed.

The result?

Well, some of the wounded game animals ran a thousand miles before dying, thus introducing their tsetse flies to areas that had never known them before. As for the bulk of the tsetse population, it moved lock, stock and barrel to the domestic livestock without losing a beat.

You Helped How?

IVORY COAST, 2002

Sports Medicine

Being slow to pay your witch doctor is just about as stupid as living anyplace that Idi Amin would call Paradise Island. But a government minister in the Ivory Coast did just that. (Well, let's be fair. Maybe his Blue Cross didn't cover it.)

It seems that more than a decade after the Ivory Coast's soccer team managed its only African Nations Cup win, the local witch doctors were finally paid. Why? Because they are convinced they helped win the trophy by means of their professional services.

Back in 1992 the minister of sport decided to provide the national team with a bit of an edge and hired the witch doctors as spiritual consultants. Named the Elephants, the team managed a narrow win during a penalty shootout in Senegal.

Fine so far—but then the sports minister kinda sorta forgot to pay the bill. The witch doctors, who live in the village of Akradio, took this oversight rather poorly. They immediately put a hex on the team. And their magic worked again—no wins for the next ten years!

Finally bowing to pressure from disappointed fans, the minister, one Moise Lida Kouassi, decided it was time to pay up. He offered humble apologies, a bottle of liquor, and two thousand dollars to the witch doctors.

There will be two signs by which we'll know if Kouassi's capitulation worked: the first will be that the Elephants win again; the second will be that his head doesn't fall off. The current odds are 6-to-5, pick 'em

You Are a Colony?
THE SPANISH AFRICAN COLONIES, 2003
The Most Recent Colonial War
Most people you talk to (except for Minister Kouassi of the Ivory Coast, who any moment now may find himself missing a head to talk with) will tell you that the age of colonialism is over, that all of Africa is independent now.

Not so. One of the oldest European colonial powers, Spain, still has several African possessions. In fact, you may recall a recent news article where five Moroccan soldiers captured a small rock of an island claimed by Spain. The next day, nine Spanish troops recaptured it, thus ending the latest colonial war in Africa.

Obviously, armies have downsized since a force of sixty Tanzanian soldiers overthrew the government of the Seychelles back in 1977.

You Cleaned How Many?
SOUTH AFRICA, 2002
African Math
"I have promised to keep his identity confidential," Jack Maxim, a spokesman for the Sandton Sun Hotel in Johannesburg, told the

Cape Times, "but I can confirm that he is no longer in our employment.

"We asked him to clean the lifts and he spent four days on the job. When I asked him why, he replied: 'Well, there are forty of them, two on each floor, and sometimes some of them aren't there.' Eventually we realized that he thought each floor had a different lift, and he'd cleaned the same two twelve times. We had to let him go. I understand he is now working for GE."

With that kind of math being exported to GE, heaven help our next generation of space shuttles.

So You're Unhappy with the Way We Run Our Airports?

KENYA, TODAY

Your Explanation Fell Flat

We'll admit that some of the cases we've discussed will stretch your credulity. Not this one. This one will throw it right out the window. Of an airplane. That isn't going anywhere. In Kenya.

"What's all the fuss about?" Weseka Sambu demanded at a hastily-convened news conference at the Jomo Kenyatta International Airport in Nairobi. "A technical hitch like this could have happened anywhere in the world. You people are not patriots. You just want to cause trouble."

So what was Sambu's problem?

He is a spokesman for Kenya Airways, and he was explaining why a flight that was to originate in Kisumu, stop in Nairobi, and then continue on to Berlin, Germany, was just a tad behind schedule.

It all began when forty-two passengers boarded the plane, ready to fly to Nairobi, when the pilot noticed that one of the tires had gone flat.

That could happen anywhere. But what came next could happen only in Africa.

First problem: Kenya Airways didn't have a spare tire at Kisumu.

Second problem: the airport's nitrogen cannister was empty, so they decided to take the tire to a local gas station for repairs.

Third problem: someone had stolen the jack and they couldn't get the wheel off—so they tried to inflate the tire with a bicycle pump.

Fourth problem: the bicycle pump didn't work, so the pilot climbed out of the plane and tried to blow into the valve with his mouth.

Fifth problem: the pilot passed out from his efforts—and the tire remained flat. For all we know, it's still flat as we write these words.

"When I announced that the flight had to be abandoned," said Sambu, "one of the passengers, a Mr. Mutu, suddenly struck me about the face with a life-jacket whistle and said we were a national disgrace. I told him he was being ridiculous and that there would be another flight in a fortnight. And in the meantime, he would be able to enjoy the scenery around Kisumu, albeit at his own expense."

Okay, now tell us how much you resent the security lines at your local airport.

You're Building What?

SOMALIA, IVORY COAST, AND DEFINITELY BOKASSA, 1990
Projects
The Italians spent $300 million building roads in Somalia. What's peculiar about that? At the time this cost came to more than $200,000 per each vehicle that existed in the entire country.

In 1990, Lilongwe, the capital city of Malawi, had a state-of-the-art television broadcast tower. What's unusual about that? Except for the Capital Hotel in Lilongwe, the Mount Soche Hotel in Blantyre, and the various palaces of President for Life Hastings Banda, there were fewer than fifty television sets in the country.

President Omar Bongo of Gabon talked the French into spending more than half a billion dollars building the most ambitious railroad on the continent. It required some fifty bridges, made with the finest hardwood, each spanning enormous canyons, but eventually it was done. What's unusual about that? Gabon's only export, the only thing they would ship to the coast aboard their state-of-the-art train, was hardwood; they used it all up building the railroad.

Remember our old pal the deposed Emperor Bokassa? Everything was going well for him until he decided to build a factory that made uniforms for the local schoolchildren. And since it was his idea, and he was the emperor, of course he owned it. What's unusual about that? Well, the average outfit cost $100, and the average family earned about $150 a year, so they were understandably reluctant to purchase the outfits. Then Bokassa passed a law— when you're the emperor passing laws is pretty easy—making it mandatory that all schoolchildren wear his company's outfits. That's when the students, most of them not yet adolescents, marched on the capital in protest. And *that's* when Bokassa decided they were an irritant and ordered them shot. And that was the beginning of the end for Bokassa.

The Ivory Coast's late President for Life, Houphouet-Boigny, ruling a country that was saddled with one of Africa's biggest per capita debts, built a huge cathedral in the capital of Abidjan. He was so pleased with it that, while rescheduling the country's debt payments, he decided to build the world's biggest church, and not in Abidjan, but in the little village of Yamoussoukro.

The structure, which was designed to dwarf St. Peter's Basilica in Rome, was about halfway up when it was finally shown off to foreign journalists in 1987. An American writer asked if it might be considered folly to build the world's biggest church in the middle of the African bush, especially when so many of the people were hungry. The guide, who had been well schooled by the 150 Frenchmen who were getting rich off the project, replied, "Don't you think there were starving and homeless people when the cornerstone was laid for Notre Dame?" End of discussion.

You Stocked the Lake with What?

KENYA, STILL

Ecology, African-Style

The Nile perch, which inhabits Lake Turkana in northern Kenya, sometimes grows to three hundred pounds. Why not, reasoned the government, capture some young ones and put them into Lake Tanganyika, the largest freshwater lake on the continent, and let them breed? Think of how much protein we can pull out of the lake in a few years to feed our hungry masses.

The Nile perch proceeded to eat almost everything else in the lake. They themselves made slow, easy targets for the thousands of crocodiles. It'll be years before the last of them is dead and the lake's balance is restored.

The same geniuses put beautiful, flowering water hyacinths into Kenya's Lake Naivasha. Why not? They were lovely, and the hippos liked eating them.

But they multiplied a *lot* faster than the lake's hippos, and on any given day 40 percent to 50 percent of the lake's surface is covered by the things.

You can go too far in the other direction. Botswana has done such a splendid job of protecting its elephant population—and word went out on the elephant grapevine, because elephants who were being decimated by poachers in Angola, Zimbabwe and Zambia migrated there—that suddenly what Botswana has is a lot of starving elephants. The Chobe National Park, which can reasonably support about 18,000 to 22,000, currently has 60,000 and the number is growing as the food supply is vanishing. But because Botswana is a signatory to the CITES Agreement—a total continentwide ban on ivory, created because other countries couldn't control their poachers—they cannot even cull their own herds and use the proceeds from the ivory to relocate some of the hungrier survivors.

Are You Crazy?

ZIMBABWE, NOT LONG AGO

See? It's Not Just Mugabe

It's generally considered that, after two decades in office, President Robert Mugabe of Zimbabwe has lost his sanity. It took him less than three years to bankrupt the country, turn a healthy populace into an army of starving beggars, and generally make himself a pariah among civilized leaders.

So why didn't the people rise up and throw him out of office?

Well, there are many reasons, including his death squads, but one reason no one has suggested to date is that it's harder to tell a Zimbabwe madman than you think.

Consider this item from a Bulawayo newspaper:

"While transporting mental patients from Harare to Bulawayo, the bus driver stopped at a roadside *shebeen* (beer hall) for a few beers. When he got back to his vehicle, he found it empty, with the twenty patients nowhere to be seen. Realizing the trouble he was in if the truth were uncovered, he halted his vehicle at the next bus stop and offered lifts to those in the queue. Letting twenty people board the bus, he then shut the doors and drove straight to the Bulawayo Mental Hospital, where he hastily handed over his 'charges,' warning the nurses that they were particularly excitable.

"Excitable was an understatement. Staff removed the furious passengers; it was three days later that suspicions were roused by the consistency of stories from the twenty. As for the real patients: nothing more has been heard of them and they have apparently blended comfortably back into Zimbabwean society. . . ."

You Are the Hope of the Future?

AFRICA, TOMORROW

What's Next?

It's hard to say. But for every Shaka Zulu, who began with a village the size of a football field and wound up with an empire three times the size of France, there's an Idi Amin, who began with a country like Uganda and is now confined to a small house thousands of miles away. For every Albert Schweitzer who devotes his life to truth, there's a South African president who tells the press that AIDS is a capitalist myth. For every Jomo Kenyatta who outlaws hunting, there's likely to be a game department officer with a unique way of eradicating tsetse flies.

But they do keep things interesting, don't they?

You Appointed Whom?

Even the most competent modern leader can't do everything. He has to appoint and trust capable and loyal subordinates. The problem comes when you put the wrong man in an important position. Nothing demonstrates this better than the tale told below.

WINSTON CHURCHILL, FIRST LORD OF THE ADMIRALTY
ENGLAND, 1914

Elizabeth Moon

In 1912, the relatively new First Lord of the Admiralty, Winston Spencer Churchill, appointed Berkeley Milne to the command of the Mediterranean Fleet. This plum of an appointment, going to a royal favorite, would have excited little comment if it had been made by a more traditional, less visionary First Lord. But Churchill? Why would an intelligent, energetic, capable young man, a man who was perfectly willing to annoy, exasperate, even infuriate traditionalists in the Royal Navy, who clearly foresaw the possibility of war with Germany, who had shown considerable strategic sense, pick Berkeley Milne for this critical post?

Admiral Milne had already impressed his fellow officers and others as the kind of blockhead who had risen to rank only by favors. He didn't want his subordinates to think or show initiative; it is not certain that he himself could do either. Certainly he could not imagine himself into the mind of the enemy, a critical ability for a senior commander in time of war. He didn't like to be interrupted at dinner by any inconvenient emergency. Affable, charming to the ladies, he had reached his highest level of competence well before this.

Jacky Fisher, heretofore enthusiastic about the young First Lord, blamed Churchill's wife, Clementine, for the appointment; he thought she had caved in to royal pressure and that Winston had caved in to Clementine. Given the character of both Winston and Clementine, and the nature of their relationship, this seems unlikely. She was not socially ambitious, and his political ambitions had already placed him higher than other young men his age. If he caved in to pressure from the royal family, it was through very different channels. Whatever the reason, this appointment put the very worst man in a critical command position on the day war broke out in 1914.

Churchill had time to repent of his decision between the appointment and the outbreak of war, but he found no way to undo it.

Milne's unsuitability showed up at the very start of the war. The Germans had one very powerful naval asset in the Mediterranean, the battle cruiser *Goeben* and her escort, the *Breslau*. She was fast, she had big guns, and she was commanded by an energetic, even brilliant, young admiral named Souchon who knew exactly how to make the best use of her. Although Germany had many fewer places to resupply in the Mediterranean than did the French and British, this ship still posed a serious threat to operations. She could (and did) shell shoreside installations; she could attack ships directly; her top speed allowed her advantages in both attack and evasion. She could outrange anything but the top British battle cruisers.

She also had weaknesses. She was coal-fueled, which meant in practice that she had a short range and needed regular coaling. She had problems with her boiler tubes that needed constant tinkering, and much of the time could not achieve her rated speed. Designed for the cold North Atlantic, she was a hellhole in the Mediterranean, with inadequate ventilation. Belowdecks, a coal-fired ship required crew to keep shifting coal about, as well as shoveling it into the insatiable maw of the boilers, to keep the ship properly ballasted—in the heat of a Mediterranean August, a hot and miserable job that left crew fainting and sick. She was a design generation behind the newest oil-fired turbine cruisers—but she had impressed both friend and enemy when she first sailed from Germany, and she certainly impressed Admiral Milne, who was convinced that she could not be successfully attacked with anything but a modern battle cruiser, of which he had only two. And, as Admiral Souchon would prove, a brilliant commander can overcome the deficiencies of slightly outmoded machines.

Churchill, even before the outbreak of war, had tried to impress on Milne the importance of keeping track of the *Goeben*. She had been up the Adriatic, getting her pesky boiler tubes worked on (Austria, of course, had Adriatic ports). But on the eve of war, she had slipped past the Adriatic Squadron and disappeared into the blue distance. Churchill sent wire after wire to Milne: find the *Goeben*. Confine her. And—when war breaks out—sink her.

Milne, like many of the navy's old guard, thought of Churchill as a hyperactive nuisance. He had too many ideas; he talked too fast and too much; he was probably unstable ... a fox-hunting cavalry officer, after all. Journalist. Politician. Self-serving publicity hound. And perhaps worst, a protégé of Jacky Fisher, while Milne was a Beresford man.

And so Milne did not hasten to the chase. Coaling—that messy, slow business—occupied some of his destroyers, and while they were at it, the battle cruisers could use a topping up, too. In a sea ringed by Allied supply bases, he chose to backtrack.

Souchon did not. He attacked the French supply bases at Phillipeville, in North Africa, thereby terrorizing the French and putting off the transport of French colonial troops from Africa to southern France. Milne, informed of this, was sure that Souchon was trying to get out into the Atlantic; he conceived that his duty was to head him off, and also to protect French shipping between Algeria and France. So he pursued, but without grasping what his enemy might be up to. His secondary fear was that Souchon would get back into the Adriatic and hole up in Trieste.

Souchon, meanwhile, was running low on coal again. Evading the British meant using every knot of his speed, and that cost coal by the ton. At this point—in the first few hours of the war—Italy was still neutral. Neither side could afford to drive Italy into the other's camp. But neutral ports could offer twenty-four hours of shelter, and fuel. Souchon hurried along the northern coast of Sicily and made it into the port of Messina, where a German collier waited.

The Straits of Messina are narrow enough that the British ships could not follow him in and blockade the port without violating Italian neutrality. Milne sat at the north end of the mousehole with two battle cruisers and assorted support craft. Milne asked the British diplomatic service to ask the Italians for permission to pass through if Souchon exited to the south, but these questions and nonanswers took longer than the twenty-four hours the *Goeben* was in port.

Watching the south end of the strait was a small British ship, the *Gloucester*. Lurking in the distance was Admiral Troubridge, with the Adriatic Squadron of aging armored cruisers and destroyers—ships clearly inferior to the *Goeben* in a fight on open water. Troubridge had the job of keeping the *Goeben* out of the Adriatic—but Souchon was not headed for the Adriatic.

Despite all the telegraphic bellowing that Churchill could put forth, nothing moved Milne to take active, useful steps to hold and sink the *Goeben*. He did not detach one of his fast battle-cruisers to go back around Sicily and be positioned in the central Mediterranean. He did not ask Troubridge to move westward and be in position to shadow or attack. He did not suggest to Troubridge—or turn Troubridge loose to think of it himself—an attack using the complicated naval topography of southern Greece, where the *Goeben* might be constrained by narrow waters into an encounter where her longer-ranged guns would be of less use.

Even when the shadowing *Gloucester* reported that the *Goeben* was moving rapidly to the east, Milne pursued in a lackadaisical manner, proving that he simply could not imagine his enemy doing anything so insane as causing real trouble in the east.

But Souchon could. And despite Turkish neutrality, he was allowed to sail the *Goeben* up the Dardanelles, and into the harbor at Constantinople, where the *Goeben*'s great guns added weight to German persuasive arguments encouraging the Turks to come into the war on the side of Austria and Germany. Some historians are sure that Turkey would have done so anyway, and that the *Goeben*'s presence made no difference. Maybe, though it's also possible that the sultan would have been glad to continue a policy of milking the various sides in turn for his lack of cooperation with the others. What is more certain is that the *Goeben*'s presence there and harrying the southern Black Sea, provided a potent barb to the bottle stopper: Russian ships could not effectively attack Constantinople.

As a result of that action, the flow of necessary supplies into Russia through Black Sea ports ceased—no guns, no butter. As a result of that action, the Germans had an inside supply line to Middle Eastern oilfields, and could also menace the Suez Canal, Britain's necessary route for transporting the armies of empire to the battlefields of Europe. As a result of Turkey's alliance with Austria and Germany, the Western Front stiffened and became one long bloodbath; Churchill's attempt to open a new front with the attack on the Dardanelles failed (partly because the traditionalists in the navy were passive-aggressively determined that it should), and with that failure, his political career went into a long eclipse. Each of these three main consequences deserves a book.

Russia's economy was perilous even before World War I started; this huge nation was more backward than any other nominally European country (most of it was in Asia, after all) and split, then as now, into many cultures, factions, religions, as well as geographic regions. It lacked the transport capacity to move large quantities of supplies by road or rail, and still depended heavily on water transport—which ran north and south along its rivers. It lacked the industrial capacity to make its own war matériel. With Austria and Germany allied against it, no shipments from the west (on efficient German railroads, for instance) could get through.

Thus, in order to arm, move and feed its huge army (and the civilians left behind), it depended on imports. Its only all-season ports were on the Black Sea, and all that shipping had to pass through the narrow Dardanelles, from the Mediterranean. Its Baltic ports were blockaded by the Germans; its Arctic ports were useful only for a brief period in summer—and Germans attacked shipping in the North Atlantic that might be headed for them. Even leaving aside the political, economic, and military consequences of the failed attack on the Dardanelles later, the loss of an all-season supply line crippled the Russian army, prevented shipments of food to alleviate famine, and contributed to the level of discontent and disorganization which—in the end—made the Revolution both inevitable and more bloody. And of course, the disorganization of the tsar's army prevented an effective Eastern Front, leaving the stagnant Western Front of trenches.

The long-term political and economic consequences of British attempts to cripple the Turks in the Near and Middle East are still with us today; the dependence on Middle Eastern oil started then, when Britain and Germany both needed it for their newer, oil-fired navies. The next war would run on oil entirely, and all combatants knew it. Whether by intimidation, cajolery, or placation, it was necessary to get the cooperation of the Near Eastern and Middle Eastern oil-producing areas; all those were tried, and all had consequences reaching into the twenty-first century. The need for oil meant growing power for oil-producing nations, and that meant a resurgence of Islam as a political power, enriching Islamic nations to a level they had not known since they exhausted the resources of the lands they had conquered a thousand years before.

Promises made then are still referred to in the bitter, angry words of today's terrorists. The philosophical alliance between anti-Jewish despots in the Near East (such as the Mufti of Jerusalem) and future Nazis started then, and through that link, to what is now a widespread intolerance in a religious culture which was, formerly, known for its tolerance. (It is difficult to imagine the great Islamic leaders of the past saying—as textbooks in some Islamic countries say now—that Jews are the cause of all their problems and should be exterminated.) Arab nationalism had already shown up (fanned in part by German agitators before World War I), but grew enormously in this period, as the British offered the same plum to win converts to their side.

Faced with Turkey's entry into the war on the side of Germany and Austria and recognizing that without supply via the Black Sea ports Russia could not mount any effective actions on the Eastern Front, Churchill conceived the bold (and, with better commanders, probably quite workable) plan to attack Turkey from the sea and reopen that vital supply line, also cutting Germany off from Middle Eastern oil. Had the plan gone forward when he wanted it to, it might well have succeeded, but it didn't. As a result, Churchill was discredited, removed from his post, and, after serving in the trenches himself, became a political outcast, remembered only as the fool who had cost so many British (and New Zealand and Australian) lives on a harebrained scheme. Without Churchill's energy, enthusiasm (sometimes misplaced but never dull), and unembarrassed patriotism, postwar England slid into apathy and depression—and eventually into appeasement, making Hitler's rise to power, and his initial military gains that much easier.

Without those years of political exile, Churchill might not have developed the character that made it possible for him to lead England in World War II—but it might not have been necessary, had he been in the government in the 1920s and 1930s. In any event, the failure in the Dardanelles changed both England and Churchill, with consequences that went far down the years ahead.

So one of the mistakes Churchill made—an uncharacteristic one for him—was to put in charge of the Mediterranean Fleet an admiral who lacked all the essential qualities needed in a naval officer in time of war.

You Traded Whom?

Sport and theater are both areas where there are actually columnists and critics to make sure nobody misses a single mistake. Which is why this may qualify to be one of the classic sports mistakes of all times.

FRAZEE AND THE BOSTON RED SOX

BOSTON, 1920

Brian M. Thomsen

Harrison Frazee had two passions in his life, baseball and the theater—not as a player or actor, mind you, or even as a fan or theatergoer.

Frazee wanted to be a world-champion baseball team owner, and a successful Broadway producer, and second best would not suffice for either.

So in 1917, Frazee bought the pennant-winning powerhouse of the American League, the Boston Red Sox, who continued their run for glory with their fourth World Series title in 1918.

Frazee knew he was buying a winner and was overjoyed when his expectations were immediately met, but unfortunately his enthusiasm did not last for long.

The following year the team began to slump and barely failed to achieve a .500 record, and the overall cost of running the team exceeded Frazee's expectations. One of the biggest expenses for the Red Sox was a former record-breaking pitcher who had entered a slump and wound up being transferred to the outfield in order to keep his still-strong (and record-breaking) bat in the lineup. The slugger slammed in twenty-nine homers that year, a new world's record at the time (partially due to his additional appearances in the lineup, since fielders could play every day, unlike pitchers).

But Frazee was not pleased. His highest-paid player was no longer making the same dominating contribution to the team in terms of defense, or more specifically pitching, as in offense, and even his slugging was suspect.

Sure he could hit the ball, but he wasn't much of a runner due to his unathletic bulk and tiny ankles.

Indeed he had to hit it out of the park in order to guarantee a home run and allow himself enough time to make it around the bases.

Sure he was a slugging superstar *now*, but who could guarantee he'd be able to keep it up? After all, he had been a pitching star too, and everyone had seen what had happened *there*!

And he ate more than the other two outfielders and the short-stop put together, with an appetite that showed no signs of waning, a fact that further dampened Frazee's enthusiasm with every road-trip food bill.

But Frazee's slackening in enthusiasm for the game was more than made up for by the growth of his enthusiasm for the stage.

He was sure that he could hear Broadway calling his name, and when a certain script came across his desk, he knew he had a hit.

It had everything—a love story, snazzy flapperesque dance numbers, and toe-tapping songs that were guaranteed to make audiences "happy" and crying for more. All it needed was a pro-ducer, and Frazee was more than happy to oblige.

There was just one small problem. . . .

Frazee's bank account.

How could he possibly continue to bankroll his team and produce his surefire hit show at the same time?

The answer was simple—he couldn't . . . until a certain gentleman from New York by the name of Colonel Jacob Ruppert, a New York brewer and entrepreneur who also just happened to own a team by the name of the New York Yankees, made him an offer he couldn't refuse.

In exchange for $125,000 cash and a promise of a $300,000 personal loan to finance the show, Ruppert was willing to take the overweight soon-to-be has-been hitter off his hands.

What a deal!

How could Frazee say no? He even stood to make a few dollars on the deal to pay off the feed-bag losses. And most important, he could finance the show that would make him a mint.

How could he refuse?

Such opportunities didn't grow on trees and unless he produced the show soon, someone else might step in, and then where would he be?

A handshake and several lawyers' conversations later, the deal was done, and all of Frazee's enthusiastic expectations about the show he wanted to produce came to fruition.

The show was *No, No, Nanette*, which became one of the biggest hits in Broadway history, making back Frazee's investment many times over, and securing him among the ranks of the most successful Broadway producers.

So Frazee got more than his money's worth for that washed-up and bloated pitcher.

Right?

Wrong.

As it turned out, that pitcher, now a fielder, still had most of his best hitting years ahead of him, hitting fifty-four homers in the next year alone (almost twice as many as his record-breaking previous year on the Red Sox), and breaking many other records over the following twelve seasons with the Yankees. And as to him being a washed up has-been pitcher, the "Babe," as he was known to his fans (or, more correctly, George Herman Ruth) pitched in only five more games (all credited wins).

Ruppert didn't buy him to pitch.

He bought him to hit, and hit he did.

He became the greatest drawing card in baseball history, guaranteeing sellouts at Yankee games home and away, building box-office and concession sales more than enough to finance twenty Broadway shows.

And to add insult to injury, Frazee's Red Sox never managed to recover their dominance.

Thus, after four pennants and four World Series championships since the team's major league inception in 1901, the Boston Red Sox did not win another pennant until 1940 and failed to win a World Series for the rest of the twentieth century.

All because of "the curse of the bambino" and a Broadway show by the name of *No, No, Nanette.*

You Created a Wonder Drug?

*In the fast-developing world of medicine we often expect near-miraculous
results. The problem is when the scientists begin to believe their own press
and fail to think through the consequences of their discoveries.*

HEINRICH DRESER

GERMANY, 1897

Edward E. Kramer

The elimination of pain has been a quest of man from the beginning of time. Early research was done using the flora and fauna
around them. In ancient times, the Mesopotamians, Greeks, and
Romans sought out fish that were able to produce electric shocks,
figuring that getting shocked by one of these fish could ease pain.
Such treatments were short in duration, and occasionally accompanied by sharp (and painful) teeth marks.

In one remedy, arthritis was treated by putting a loose bag over
the affected arm or leg, filling the bag with the dirt and ants from
an ant bed, then tying the bag shut so the ants couldn't escape. The
arm or leg was left in the bag for two or three hours while the ants
bit the patient. Another remedy for arthritis involved daily bee
stings.

Plants were popular sources of pain remedies in just about
every culture on earth. Leaves, roots and bark were boiled and
beaten and ground into teas, pastes, poultices, and ointments to

ease the pain that afflicted everyone at one time or another. The white poppy provided one of the strongest painkillers in nature's pharmacy. Its unripe seeds were dried to produce a "juice," or in Greek—opium. The first reference to opium in history appears in the writings of Theophrastus in the third century B.C.E.

Arabian traders introduced the drug to the Orient, where it was employed mainly for the control of dysentery. In the fourth century, Hilary, the bishop of Poitiers, was exiled to the Orient by the emperor Constantius. It was there that he first wrote about drugs that lulled the soul to sleep. Apuleius, a compiler of medical literature in the fifth century, wrote of the drug "if anyone is to have a limb mutilated, burnt, or sawn, he may drink a half ounce with wine, and whilst he sleeps the member may be cut off without any pain or sense."

After the collapse of the Roman Empire in the fifth century, science took a backseat to religion. The soul was viewed as far more important than the body, and medical treatment virtually vanished. Hospitals became places where the sick were cared for, until they recovered or died. Many classic Greek and Roman medical texts were destroyed because they were seen as heretical.

In the mid-to late-1800s, opium became a fairly popular drug. Opium dens were scattered throughout what we know today as the Wild West. The opium influx during this period was due in large part to the drug being brought into the country via Chinese immigrants who came here to work on the railroads.

While American history places famous cowboys of the period, like Wild Bill Hickok and Kit Carson, in the taverns of the Wild West, they actually frequented opium dens more often than saloons. It was not uncommon for the cowhands to spend several days and nights at a time in these dens in a constant dream state, as they became physically addicted to the drug. Eventually, opium was even promoted as a cure for alcoholism.

In 1803, German pharmacist Friedrich Serturner isolated and described an opium alkaloid that he named morphine, after the Greek god of dreams, Morpheus. It was considered a wonder drug because it eliminated severe pain associated with medical operations or traumatic injuries. It left the user in a completely numb euphoric dream state.

By the mid-1850s morphine was available throughout the United States and became important to the medical profession. Other opiate derivatives such as codeine and papervine were also used. The benefits of using the drug to treat severe pain were considered nothing short of remarkable to doctors of the time. Unfortunately, the addictive properties of the drug went virtually unnoticed until after the Civil War.

During the war, morphine was doled out like candy by army surgeons, who were surrounded by suffering and had few remedies to offer. Nearly 10 million opiate pills were issued to Union soldiers, along with 2.8 million ounces of other opium-based preparations. Morphine was used to treat not just wounds but chronic campaign diseases such as diarrhea, dysentery, and malaria.

It became even more popular after the war as invalided veterans sought relief from constant pain. By the end of the nineteenth century, there were roughly 200,000 morphine addicts in the United States. Because of the drug's source, morphine addiction was commonly called the army disease. Doctors became perplexed and were completely in the dark as to how to treat this new epidemic.

In 1874, an English research chemist, C. R. Allder-Wright, working at St. Mary's Hospital in London, boiled morphine with acetic acid over a stove for several hours to produce diacetylmorphine, a white, odorless, bitter crystalline powder. After feeding the new drug to his dogs, he noted that it induced "great prostration, fear, sleepiness speedily following the administration and a slight tendency to vomiting," and decided to discontinue his experiments.

In 1897, chemist Felix Hoffmann of the Bayer Company of Elberfeld, Germany, discovered a new process for modifying salicyclic acid to produce acetylsalicyclic acid (ASA). This compound had been isolated before as a remedy for fever and inflammation, and the healing powers of salicylates (derived from willow bark) had been known for centuries. Hoffmann, however, had created a reliable process for making it.

Heinrich Dreser directed product development for Bayer, where he was in charge of testing the efficacy and safety of new drugs. He was admired for his thorough, methodical approach, and for his innovations in testing. Dreser was, in fact, the first chemist to use animal experimentation on an industrial scale. He had also negotiated a special deal with Bayer that guaranteed him a share of the profits from products he launched.

Dreser tested this new drug (later to be named aspirin) but, after cursory consideration, rejected it. Ostensibly, his objection was that ASA would have an "enfeebling" action on the heart. "The product has no value," he determined. Diacetylmorphine was also synthesized in the Bayer laboratory by Hoffmann, two weeks after he first synthesized ASA. The work was initiated by Dreser, who was already aware of Allder-Wright's earlier research, even though he subsequently implied that diacetylmorphine was an original Bayer invention.

By early 1898, Dreser tested diacetylmorphine on sticklebacks, frogs and rabbits. He also tested it on some of Bayer's workers and on himself. The workers loved it, some saying it made them feel "heroic" (*heroisch*). This was also the term used by chemists to describe any strong drug. Chemists had been looking for some time for a non-addictive substitute for morphine. If diacetylmorphine could be shown to be such a product, Dreser would be rich.

Creating a brand name was easy. By November of 1898, Dreser had presented the new drug—Heroin—to the Congress of German Naturalists and Physicians, claiming it was ten times more effective as a cough medicine than codeine but had only a tenth of its toxic effects. He told them it was also more effective than morphine as a painkiller, that it was safe, and that it wasn't habit-forming.

At the time, tuberculosis and pneumonia were then the leading causes of death, and even routine coughs and colds could be severely incapacitating. Heroin, which both depresses respiration and, as a sedative, gives a restorative night's sleep, seemed a miracle solution. In its initial release, Heroin had over four times the potency of the morphine from which it was derived.

Dreser had written about Heroin in leading medical journals, and studies had endorsed his view of it as an effective treatment in asthma, bronchitis, phthisis and tuberculosis. The Bayer Company mailed out thousands of free samples to physicians in Europe and the United States. The label on the side displayed a lion and a globe, along with the Bayer name.

By 1899, Bayer had already produced a ton of Heroin and had exported the new drug to twenty-three countries. Because of the large population of morphine addicts in the United States, a craze for patent medicines, and a relatively lax regulatory framework,

Heroin became an immediate hit. Manufacturers of cough syrup were soon lacing their products with Bayer Heroin.

Bayer never advertised Heroin to the general public, at whom they targeted their consumer drug, Bayer Aspirin. However, the samples and brochures directed at the physicians stated: "Heroin: the Sedative for Coughs . . . order a supply from your jobber." Soon, there were Heroin pastilles, cough lozenges, tablets, water-soluble salts and elixirs. The drug's popularity encouraged imitators, and a St. Louis pharmaceutical company offered a "Sample Box Free to Physicians" of its "Dissolve on the Tongue Antikamnia & Heroin Tablets."

"It possesses many advantages over morphine," wrote the *Boston Medical and Surgical Journal* in 1900. "It's not hypnotic, and there's no danger of acquiring a habit." The philanthropic Saint James Society in the United States. mounted a campaign to supply free samples of Heroin through the mail to morphine addicts who were trying to give up their habits. But worrying rumors were surfacing.

In 1902, when Heroin sales were accounting for roughly 5 percent of Bayer's net profits, both French and American researchers were reporting cases of "heroinism" and addiction. In the next three years, at least 180 clinical papers on Heroin were published around the world—most of them favorable. The American Medical Association then approved Bayer Heroin for general use and advised that it be used "in place of morphine in various painful infections."

There had been an explosion of Heroin-related admissions at New York and Philadelphia hospitals, and in East Coast cities a substantial population of recreational users was reported. Many supported their habits by collecting and selling scrap metal, hence the name "junkie." In another year, the use of Heroin without a prescription was outlawed in the United States. By 1913, with prohibition inevitable, the Bayer Company decided to stop production. Other companies, however, continued production of the drug.

The growing dimensions of heroin addiction finally convinced authorities that heroin's liabilities outweighed its medical merits, and in 1924 both houses of Congress unanimously passed legislation outlawing the import or manufacture of heroin. The deputy police commissioner of New York reported that 94 percent of all drug addicts arrested for various crimes were heroin users. In Britain, however, the medical use of heroin continues to this day, accounting for 95 percent of the world's legal heroin consumption.

Heinrich Dreser, himself addicted to the drug he pioneered, died four days before Christmas in 1924. The cause of death was given as a cerebral apoplexy, or stroke. Dreser, incorrigible in his misjudgment, had spent his twilight years taking a daily dose of the wrong wonder drug. Had anyone known at the time, it was conceivable that he could have averted that fate by taking a daily dose of the drug he rejected for its lack of medical value—the Bayer Aspirin.

You Sold Whom for How Much?

It is amazing what hard work, perseverance, and schoolboy friendship can sometimes accomplish.

Brian M. Thomsen

Jerry Siegel and Joe Shuster (both born in 1914) first met at Glenville High School in Cleveland in 1931. Joe, a budding cartoonist wannabe, had just moved there from Toronto and in meeting Jerry realized that he was in the presence of a kindred soul. Both were unathletic, bespectacled, shy, and, most important, science fiction fans.

Jerry had been submitting stories to the pulps for quite a while. He longed to have his work in print right alongside those of his favorite authors, but his efforts had yielded no success and even less encouragement. Undaunted, the aspiring young writer joined forces with his illustrator buddy and started their own amateur magazine, entitled *Science Fiction—The Advance Guard of Future Civilization,* as a venue for both of their talents, which heretofore had been underappreciated by the marketplace. In their January 1933 issue a story by Herbert S. Fine (Siegel under a pen name) was featured entitled "The Reign of the Superman," complete with illustrations by Shuster. It was a Frankenstein sort of tale that illustrated the age-old axiom that absolute power corrupts absolutely. Their magazine expired soon thereafter, but the concept of "the super-man" stayed with them for further noodling on the storyboards.

Roughly about this time M. C. Gaines was pioneering a new magazine genre with his publication *Famous Funnies*, which collected comic strips into book/magazine form. The two cartoonist wannabes decided to give this art a try and began to develop their concept of a Superman character (without "super strength" or other powers outside of the normal pulp genre) into a comic strip story, which they submitted to Gaines in 1933. Unfortunately, as luck would have it, Gaines had to turn it down since he was only collecting strips that were already appearing in print and at the time was not interested in considering any original submissions.

Siegel and Shuster were undaunted and continued to put their "Superman" on submission to the various funny-book publishers and syndicators that began popping up with greater though usually short-lived frequency. Unfortunately, rejections abounded, even from Super Magazines Inc., which should have been a natural home for their concept. Still, their work was being considered, and eventually in 1935 they made their first professional sale to National Allied Publishing—but not the Superman project.

Meanwhile M. C. Gaines still remembered the young team and in 1937 reestablished contact with them, soliciting some new projects. Through his contacts they wound up visiting several New York publishers and eventually found themselves in the offices of an operation called *Detective Comics* run by Harry Donenfeld and Jack Liebowitz, for whom they had previously done some work on a series called "Slam Bradley." Donenfeld and Liebowitz asked Gaines if he would mind letting them take over on Siegel and Schuster's "Superman" project for the upcoming launch of *Action Comics*.

Gaines was not in a position to move with the property himself, so he gave them his blessing and as a result, Donenfeld and Liebowitz made a modest offer for the property that had been lying fallow since the boys had first tried to get a door into the industry.

Siegel and Shuster were overjoyed. Their years of work were finally going to be rewarded. *Detective Comics* was already a success, and the same publishing formula was going to be applied to *Action Comics*.

How could they lose?

Donenfeld and Liebowitz realized that there were a great many risks involved. The funny-book business was tough, and even the best idea was never a sure thing, so in exchange for their trying out this new idea and the princely sum of $130, Siegel and Shuster gave them the thirteen-page story that would be featured on the cover of *Action Comics #1*, as well as the legal ownership of the character featured. They also realized that if their creation took off, both of them would soon be seeing plenty of work for new adventures, and possible strip circulation for the series.

Siegel and Shuster believed in Superman's potential, and they were right! By 1939, the character got his own eponymous comic; in 1940 he made his radio debut, then his first appearance as a toy figure; and in 1942 it was picked up by the Mutual Network, who aired the fifteen-minute show three days a week. As National Comics (now called DC) carefully nurtured the exploitation of these rights (including motion-picture and cartoon opportunities), Siegel and Shuster continued to do quite well, with individual incomes from their work on the property (according to Siegel and Shuster) of $30,000 per annum, which by today's standards would be roughly the equivalent of $315,000 a year apiece.

In 1947, the two creators decided that they weren't satisfied with their original agreement with Donenfeld and Liebowitz. Superman's popularity had suffered a slight postwar decline, while other comic genres (in which DC also had an interest) were in ascendancy. Siegel and Shuster viewed DC's other lines as competition that was cutting into their own income, were chagrined over their lack of control of the property, and resentful of Donenfeld and Liebowitz reaping the lion's share of the revenues their creation had produced. So they decided to sue for $5 million and the return of all rights to their creation.

But a contract was a contract, and that was good enough for the courts. Though no one could have realized at the time how *big* the Superman property would become, Donenfeld and Liebowitz had indeed paid fair market value for it at the time (it had, after all, been floating and rejected all over town for years prior to their acquisition) and had made a substantial investment into its publication beyond the monies paid to the creators, and because of this investment Siegel and Shuster had also reaped substantial fiscal benefits over the years.

Eventually the courts decided that indeed the creators had legally assigned all rights to the character to the publishers. A settlement was reached where the two creators received $100,000 (most of which was probably eaten up by legal fees). They parted ways with DC (a reconciliation not to take place for over twenty-five years) and signed with Magazine Enterprises to launch a new character named Funnyman, a venture that was dead after only six issues.

DC, however, continued to nurture the property with numerous motion pictures, TV shows, and even a Broadway musical, making Superman one of America's most successful pop culture icons.

You're Out of Tune

There once was a time when celebrity alone was enough to breathe success into the recording industry. Now it seems more important to them to blame downloading students for the decline of their sales rather than deal with cost and quality questions. But such an attitude is hardly new.

THE RECORD INDUSTRY
UNITED STATES, 1950 ON (AND ON, AND ON)

Brian M. Thomsen

Movie stars from Robert Mitchum to Jimmy Durante to even Walter Brennan enjoyed top-forty success with both singles and albums, and teeny-bopper stars like Frankie Avalon and Pat Boone paved the way for similar successes by lesser melodious talents like Shelley Fabares and Ed "Kookie" Byrnes that quickly became one-hit wonders.

As the public became more fickle and celebrities more numerous and, indeed, less talented, the onetime negative onus of being a one-hit wonder was soon replaced by no-hit wonders, and even worse, truly bad singers with even worse albums.

For every folksy success by a TV star such as Leonard Nimoy or David Soul there were truly bad and embarrassing efforts by other TV stars such as Jack Webb and William Shatner.

Likewise the spoken-word ruminations of Richard Harris and Rod McKuen, whose heartfelt rendering of lyrics, if not melodious,

were at least soulful, were countered by such truly ill-inspired executions as Sebastian Cabot's (Mr. French of *Family Affair*) renditions of the lyrics of Bob Dylan.

There was even a record of Tony Randall and Jack Klugman
(from TV's *Odd Couple*) singing duets à la their Oscar and Felix
characters, which included a comic off-key version of the Carly
Simon hit "You're So Vain."

As singers, most of these performers were pretty good actors.

But even professional singers can occasionally make dubious
decisions.

In the seventies a beer company (later followed by a soda company) sponsored a series of low-cost concerts in New York's
Central Park with a wide selection of acts, usually pairing a
promising newcomer as the opener with an established crowd
pleaser. Bands such as the Beach Boys and the Ojays might sometimes be on the same schedule with Leon Redbone, Johnny Cash,
or Perry Como, thus offering the public a taste of something that
would appeal to almost every diverse appetite.

One of the headliners one year was Canadian songbird Anne
Murray, whose "Snowbird" was a top-forty standard of the AM
radio set and who had already built a substantial audience among
the country-and-western market as well. True, New York was not
known as a C&W (or AM radio, for that matter) demographic, but
nonetheless Anne was confident that her fans would follow her
anywhere and turn out in droves.

As per the mix-and-match nature of the schedule, her opening
act was aimed at a slightly tougher, more hip demographic, and
wound up being a promising young talent from the Jersey Shore
who had a couple of albums under his belt and a new one sched-

uled for release just prior to the concert date. Though Anne was unsure if his music would appeal to her audience, she quickly figured that no harm could be done, and if her audience knew that they didn't like his music, they would either show up late and miss the opening act or grin and bear it until she came on.

With less than two weeks to go before the concert a strange thing happened. The rocker who was to be her opening act wound up on the cover of both *Time* and *Newsweek* with headlines proclaiming that he was the future of rock and roll, and overnight this guy from New Jersey by the name of Bruce Springsteen was to New York audiences the second coming of Elvis.

The promoters of the concert were in a quandary.

All of a sudden the opening act was bigger than the headliner.

They quickly approached Anne's manager with a proposal: What if she was to go on first?

The manager listened to their arguments and consulted with his client, and quickly returned to them with a cordial no. Anne was the headliner, she was the draw, and that's just the way it was.

On the night of the concert Springsteen took the stage—and wound up staying the night. Anne's people saw the crowd had gone wild with enthusiasm for this rocker and concluded that his fans had shown up instead of hers, and rather than have her perform to a less-than-appreciative audience (if not one that might be openly hostile, having been disappointed at the curtailment of encores for the opening act), she ceded the stage to him. That discretion was probably the better part of valor.

Anne Murray quietly left the park's backstage area without performing.

* * *

Another dubious pursuit of the musical set involves reinvention, whereby the singer-musician actively pursues a widening of audience by incorporating more diverse material in their repertoire.

Sometimes it works, such as Keith Emerson of ELP doing a classical concerto, Sinead O'Connor's torch-song classic follow-up to her cutting-edge debut album, or even Pat Boone's little bit of leather and metal renditions of hard rock classics.

Other times . . . not so much.

Perhaps the most noticeable recent example of this involved one of the top-selling recording artists of the nineties.

Garth Brooks was a country-and-western phenomenon with crossover appeal, with album sales dwarfing the competition across the country.

Garth was bigger than Johnny Cash, John Denver, and Loretta Lynn all rolled into one. But he wanted to try something different.

Enter Chris Gaines, or rather, enter Garth Brooks as Chris Gaines, a fictional Australian rocker bedecked in Goth gear and makeup from the cosmetologist who designed the look for Brandon Lee in *The Crow*, with a sound produced by pop mogul Babyface and Don Was (formerly of new wave group Was/Was Not). He would be Garth's alter ego, master a new sound, and attract a new audience. He would even appear as a musical guest on *Saturday Night Live,* as if Chris Gaines and Garth Brooks were not the same person.

The result—the worst-selling Garth Brooks album in a decade, a record that turned off new fans as well as old.

Garth Brooks is a tremendous talent in his field, but he was as good a rocker as he was a baseball player . . . and that is yet another story worthy of this volume.

You Executed All the What?

One of the classic cartoon jokes is the character sawing off the tree limb he is standing on. This is less funny when the leader of a major nation does just about the same thing to his entire country.

RUSSIA, 1937–1942

Bill Fawcett

Brutal despots who kill large numbers of their own people are rarely well remembered. Few today have a warm spot for Caligula or Vlad the Impaler. Perhaps one of the worst of these throughout all of history was Joseph Stalin. He was heartless, paranoid, and disloyal to an extreme. But not only wasn't he a nice guy, it can be easily seen that he was also a rather lousy dictator. Even Idi Amin had some followers left when he fled Africa. Soviet Russia literally named their new social policy in the 1950s de-Stalinization. Why? Because strangely enough, though Stalin held power for several decades in Russia, as a national leader he was often grossly incompetent, or at least incredibly shortsighted and perhaps personally a coward.

Okay, so you run Russia with an iron hand. The members of the politburo are all your appointees. Last year, when your close friend and heir apparent, Kirov, disagreed with you on a matter of foreign policy, you had him assassinated. Then you blamed the assassination on your few political opponents left in the

Communist Party and had them killed as well. Now you stand unchallenged as head of the government and the party. You control the economy, the farms, the factories and the secret police (NKVD).

The only other entity in all Russia with any power at all is the Red Army. The officers of the army are generals who have stood by for years and followed your orders without question. The ones who had questions normally finished asking them to a firing squad. This is the Red Army, which is also the only defense against the growing power of a Nazi-led Germany.

So they have not shown any tendency to involve themselves in party politics or challenge you as dictator. And, having alienated every possible ally because they are capitalists, you need the Red Army. Even so, they could be a threat, so . . . too bad.

In June of 1937 the eight top officers of the Red Army were accused of plotting a coup against "the Party," which meant Stalin. All eight were quickly convicted and executed. These executions, though, caused unrest in the ranks of the other officers. It certainly would not put them at ease or make them feel secure. At the very least, being a good paranoid, Stalin realized that he had just created several openings for ambitious men—the very sort of officers that might challenge him in later years. But no worry, he just eliminated them too. In fact, he simply made the criteria for execution any real sign of competence, initiative, or any other trait that would make someone a good officer. After all, if the officer corps is all dull bricks unwilling or unable to do more than obey specific orders, it will be no threat.

In the last half of 1937 and into 1938 over 30,000 officers and noncommissioned officers were executed. The Red Army most certainly ceased to be a threat to Stalin. It also effectively ceased being a threat to Germany, Finland or anyone else. One irony of the entire officer purge is that there is some evidence the purported military coup was actually generated by German intelligence and was not valid. But Stalin was too paranoid to care.

Incidentally, for good measure, Stalin then appointed a new head to the NKVD, and this man, Beria, then executed everyone who had been in a position of authority during the purges of either the army or the party. Those competent enough to execute anyone else marginally competent or creative were now also no longer a threat.

Since he couldn't consider defeating the Nazis, Stalin did an about-face and, after characteristically purging his entire Foreign Office, signed the infamous non-aggression pact with Germany in 1939. This meant that Stalin had sold out Europe but had gotten himself a few years of peace in which to rebuild the Red Army. So then, a few months later, the dictator looked around and decided Finland, all two million or so Finns, were a threat to almost 100 million people of the Soviet Union because their border was near Leningrad. And when Stalin asked them, they "unreasonably" refused to allow the stationing of Soviet troops inside large portions of their country. So less than a year after destroying all of the leadership, Stalin's army was invading Finland. A year later, and after losing more men than were in the entire Finnish army, Stalin finally forced the Finns to cede the lands near Leningrad and drove them to become the reluctant but close allies of Nazi Germany. Stalin now had his secure border but had lost many more of the few experienced military officers he had missed in the purge.

It is now 1941. Stalin has watched Germany overrun Poland,

destroy France in weeks, and seen Rommel drive the British halfway across northern Africa. An entire chapter in *Mein Kampf* speaks of the need to cleanse the east of the Russians and their allies. But they have a non-aggression pact. Stalin was soon sent information from his own agents and those of the Allies that Germany was planning to attack the Soviet Union that summer. Winston Churchill sent a personal message directly to Joseph Stalin with details of the invasion. The top Soviet spy, Sorge, also reported that an attack was imminent. Stalin, not paranoid enough for the first time in years, decided it was a plot by the Western powers to get him to attack Germany. Hmmm, okay, maybe he was just too paranoid after all.

Operation Barbarossa comes as a complete shock to the Soviet dictator. So he disappears for two full weeks, leaving the state and army to flounder. Remember what happens to those who show initiative? You only obey orders, Stalin's orders, but Joseph Stalin is nowhere to be seen. Several million casualties and several thousand square miles of occupied land later, Stalin reappears and begins organizing. He also begins searching for scapegoats to blame for the failure of an army, which he recently decapitated and which was left without top leadership for two weeks after being attacked by the strongest military force in the world, for not stopping the German attack at the border. Yep, more experienced leaders are shot, those few not captured by the Wehrmacht anyhow.

Nothing should detract from the incredible sacrifices and courage shown by the Russian peoples in eventually defeating the Nazis at the cost of tens of millions dead. No one just after the war had the nerve to stop Stalin from falsifying the internal history to show how the dictator had personally saved the nation. But there is little doubt that Stalin personally—and with probably no malice aforethought, as there seems to have been no forethought at all and maybe a bit of cowardice—put the Red Army and Soviet Union in a position that ensured the early victories of the Panzer armies.

You Built It Where?

An old proverb says to never attribute to intent what can be explained by ignorance. Then again, in the cases of corporate greed, you can't also rule out almost total stupidity and the power of short-range thinking.

HOOKER CHEMICALS AND THE LOVE CANAL SCHOOL BOARD
NEW YORK, 1953

Paul Kupperberg

Love was in the air in the city of Niagara Falls, New York. As well as in the soil. And the groundwater, and buried beneath the public school, and seeping into the basements of homes.

This was a gift of Love, but not the kind of love that every year brings honeymooners by the tens of thousands to the most famous and spectacular waterfall in the world. This is the legacy of the Love Canal, a neighborhood in the southeast LaSalle district of the city. The area takes its name from a small parcel of land approximately sixty feet wide and three thousand feet long, less an actual canal than the first section of a planned seven-mile waterway to route waters from the Niagara River around Niagara Falls and provide water and hydroelectric power for a planned model industrial city.

William T. Love had set out to create a literal Utopia in upstate New York, "the most perfect city in existence," he boasted to all who would listen. A city to house a million people, powered by unlimited electricity generated by the thundering waters of the falls, bankrolled by industry taking advantage of the abundant electrical power, and with thousands of acres set aside to be "the most extensive and beautiful (parkland) in the world."

But the model city never happened. Though ground was broken in 1893 and a small section of the canal dug, events of the day conspired against its completion.

Instead, William Love's dream of Utopia wound up paving the way for one of the most famous man-made ecological disasters of all time.

The entire history of the Love Canal is plagued by one puzzling decision after another, starting with the one to use the big hole in the ground within the Niagara Falls city limits as a toxic waste dump in 1920 and reaching the height of absurdity with the brilliant notion to build a public school directly on top of the site. It is a story of bold negligence, with the company that sold the Love Canal site to the city making no attempt to conceal what it was doing, blithely washing its hands of the chemical waste buried a few feet underground with disclaimers absolving them of any future liability. With so many bad choices made across so many years, it's hard to point the finger of blame for this ecological disaster at any single source.

William T. Love, at least, had undertaken his visionary venture with only the loftiest of goals in mind. In the last years of the nineteenth century, electricity was opening the industrializing United States to an entire new world of potential. The Niagara River, flowing between the United States and Canada and ending in the thunderously spectacular falls shared by the two nations, provided ample resources for the generation of electrical power: a continuous cascade of water to turn massive generators. Generating plants had been built along the river for years, providing power to the electrochemical and electrometallurgical firms that flooded into the area. But while the technology of the day allowed for the generation of cheap power, it had not yet come up with an efficient or cost-effective means of transmitting the power over any great distance. In order to have access to the quantities of cheap power, customers had to be located close to the source.

Love saw his "model city" becoming "one of the greatest manufacturing cities in the United States . . . Nothing approaching it in magnitude, perfection or power has ever before been attempted." At the heart of his plan was the canal to divert water from the Niagara, "capturing the mighty force of the water as it sped into the rapids before rushing over the huge drop."

With colorful and hyperbolic brochures, Love lured investors and backers to his plan. On paper, in theory, it made perfect sense, but the combination of a mid-1890s economic downturn, a congressional resolution against the diversion of Niagara's waters, and Louis Tesla's discovery of how to cheaply and efficiently transmit electricity over great distances by means of an alternating current killed Love's plan in the cradle. Factories no longer needed to be concentrated near the falls to have access to cheap power.

William T. Love and his city were soon forgotten.

Except for the big hole he had left behind. Over the years, rainwater collected in the great ditch and it found new life as a recreational area, with swimming in the summer and ice skating in the winter. Not a bad fate for a parcel of land that was once intended to sit at the heart of Utopia.

But in 1920, the land was sold at public auction and turned from playground to dumping ground, becoming a municipal and chemical disposal site. In 1927, the city of Niagara Falls annexed the village of LaSalle and the Love Canal. Then, in 1942, the Hooker Chemical and Plastics Corporation (now Occidental Chemical) bought the Love Canal site. Section by section, Hooker Chemical drained the canal, lined it with a thick layer of clay, and began using it as a dump for hundreds of barrels of electrochemical byproducts, not to mention a toxic stew of municipal waste products. By 1953, Hooker Chemical had filled the twenty- to twenty-five-foot-deep pit to maximum capacity with an estimated 22,000 tons of toxic waste. A thick clay cap, several layers of dirt, and a layer of sod atop the filled canal was the only shield between the lethal chemical cocktail and the growing Niagara Falls community.

Contrary to contemporary attitudes, it wasn't unusual at the time for communities to willingly accept a chemical waste dump in a residential area. The chemical industry was held in high regard in the 1940s, celebrated for the medical and lifestyle advances it was making possible. A large number of Niagara Falls residents were themselves employed by the many chemical companies around the city and were proud of their association with an industry that brought the future home today. No one believed that so forward a thinking industry would engage in practices hazardous to the public health. In addition, few in those days realized that there was even a link between exposure to chemical waste and such health problems as cancer, birth defects, and liver damage. Indeed, Hooker Chemical's experts were convinced that the clay lining and cap of the canal would be more than adequate to contain the mess it had left belowground.

In May 1953, the most unbelievable chapter in the Love Canal story took place when the Niagara Falls Board of Education bought the contaminated parcel of land from Hooker Chemical.

There were those who claimed, as early as 1948, to have discovered a link between discarded insecticides and cancer. One such scientist, Dr. Robert Mobbs of Boston, scoffed at Hooker's later claims that, in the 1940s, they had no reason to suspect these wastes were hazardous. "They ignored, minimized, and suppressed the facts," Dr. Mobbs charged. If Hooker Chemical was, as they were to claim, unaware of the hazards, why then did they go to such great pains to include a carefully worded disclaimer in the deal that gave the covered site to the Niagara Falls Board of Education for the price of $1? Not that the board wasn't thrilled to get the land: the postwar baby boom had left the city in desperate need of new schools. Parents in the LaSalle district in particular were pushing for a school closer to home. On the face of it, Hooker Chemical's offer seemed like a dream come true. They just made sure that, going forward, their hands would be clean of blame and that the board of education would assume "all risks and liabilities," and that "no claim, suit, action or demand of any nature whatsoever shall ever be made (by the Board) . . . for injury to a person or persons, including death resulting therefrom, or loss of or damage to property caused by reason of the presence of said industrial wastes."

In spite of warnings from one of their lawyers, the school board signed off on the deal, and in 1955 four hundred students began attending the newly constructed 99th Street Elementary School. The school had no basement or swimming pool; though seemingly unconcerned that the structure sat atop a lake of lethal sludge, the builders knew enough not to dig too deep and risk disturbing or damaging the barrels of waste.

Soon after, houses were being built on the fringes of the dump site, a neighborhood growing up around this fouled area. Though what lay beneath the surface was common knowledge, homeowners were not warned of the potential hazards percolating beneath their streets. But soon, children were wearing handkerchiefs over their faces to block out the smells as they walked to school. Chunks of phosphorus had worked their way up from the underground dump to become playthings called "fire rocks" by kids who liked to make them explode in a shower of sparks by throwing them against the ground. Children were being burned by waste that began oozing to the surface in yards and playgrounds. By 1976, the odors and waste seepage had reached disastrous proportions. Unusually heavy rain and snowfalls over the previous two years had caused the groundwater level to rise, forcing the waste to the surface, contaminating ponds and other surface water, including the Niagara River itself. Poisonous sludge giving off fumes that caused nausea and headaches was oozing into basements and sump pumps installed to drain it were quickly eaten away by chemical corrosion. Increasingly noxious fumes caused the paint on some homes to turn black. Muddy ditches burned children's skin or covered them in strange oily substances, while trees and gardens slowly blackened and died.

And, most ominously, the Love Canal district suffered an unusually high number of birth defects, incidents of cancer, and nervous system disorders. A study of women in a certain age group showed that more than 35 percent of them had experienced spontaneous abortions, far in excess of the national average. Children were born with cleft palates, eye problems, deafness, and retardation, among other congenital defects. Studies by the Agency for Toxic Substances and Disease Registry showed an incredible 418 different chemicals in the air, soil, and water of the Love Canal area, including deadly concentrations of benzene, a known carcinogen.

Finally, in April of 1978, after years of crusading by the editors of the Niagara Falls *Gazette* and demonstrations by residents, New York's health commissioner, Robert Whalen, declared the Love Canal a threat to the public health and safety. The area around the landfill itself was fenced off and the 99th Street School closed. Whalen further recommended that all pregnant women and children be evacuated from the immediate area. In August of the same year, New York governor Hugh Carey announced that the state would purchase two hundred houses located in the worst of the contaminated area. On August 7, President Jimmy Carter ordered the Federal Disaster Assistance Agency to provide emergency financial aid to the stricken area, the first time emergency funds had been approved for something other than a natural disaster. The Love Canal was eventually declared a Federal Disaster Area in order to qualify for additional federal aid.

What followed was years of upheaval, relocation, and tests, as well as efforts on behalf of the state and federal governments to clean up the mess left behind by Hooker Chemical. In spite of the company's efforts to distance itself from liability, more than eight hundred lawsuits totaling $11 billion were filed against Hooker, the city of Niagara Falls, and the Board of Education by 1979. In March of 1979, a company vice president testified before a Senate subcommittee that Hooker Chemical had no legal liability for the Love Canal disaster. In December of that year, the Federal Justice Department filed a $124 million lawsuit against Hooker, and in 1989, New York State initiated a $635 million suit against Hooker's parent company, Occidental Petroleum, charging them with responsibility for the disaster. Through it all, Hooker Chemical continued denying culpability.

In the end, almost one thousand families were evacuated and relocated. Four different chemicals suspected of causing cancer were found in the air. EPA testing of thirty-six people in the Love Canal uncovered eleven cases of chromosome damage. The courts would be tied up for years with lawsuits, while state and federal agencies would pour hundreds of millions of dollars into the cleanup and reclamation efforts.

Today, the Love Canal remains surrounded by a fence and the cleanup and reclamation efforts continue. For all its efforts at deniability, Hooker Chemical's role in this environmental catastrophe was undeniable and the company has had to pay more than $129 million of the cleanup bill. According to the Environmental Protection Agency, "numerous toxic chemicals had migrated into the surrounding area directly adjacent to the original landfill . . . run-off drained into the Niagara River . . . (and) dioxin and other contaminants migrated from the landfill to the existing sewers."

As a result of the Love Canal controversy and publicity, Niagara Falls identified three more Hooker Chemical dump sites in Niagara Falls containing over a million tons of toxic waste. Another estimated 250 smaller waste disposal sites are believed to exist within three miles of the Niagara River. Legislation passed in the wake of the disaster has created such boons as the Resource Conservation and Recovery Act and the Super Fund laws. Both laws were designed to force industry to place the safety and well-being of the public and the environment first, making the companies that generate hazardous wastes responsible for them from "cradle to grave" and to root out and clean up existing trouble spots.

While it may be argued that Hooker Chemical acted not out of malice but ignorance of the time bomb it had left buried beneath the ground in the Love Canal—and, incredibly, some have argued just that—the aftermath of this well-publicized disaster brought about some good. It created greater public awareness of chemical waste dumping and provided the funds for cleaning up contaminated sites.

And, most important, it made certain that some future Hooker Chemical company would not be leaving a Love Canal of tomorrow sitting atop a cesspool of death.

You Choose Whom?

Some compromises work better than others. Other times decisive action is required. Occasionally by mistake the former is actually the decisive latter, and what was mistakenly thought to be a compromise opens the door to something very different from what was expected. Here is one compromise that definitely has some major and unexpected results.

THE ELECTION OF JOHN XXII
THE VATICAN, 1958

Brian M. Thomsen

On October 9, 1958, after numerous long illnesses, Pope Pius XII expired at Castel Gandolfo, and immediately the search for his successor was begun by various Vatican power brokers. The actual and thought to be secret election process was clearly laid out by Church law, and was thought to be governed by divine intervention rather than internal Church politics, but as the Good Book reminds us, sometimes "the Lord works in mysterious way," and even more so in situations regarding political wheeling and dealing.

Pius XII's was not the most popular of papacies. He had succeeded Pius XI (under whom he had served as secretary of state) in 1939, and though he may not have been anti-Semitic and pro-Nazi, as recent allegations seem to contend, it is obvious that this wartime pope favored quiet forms of diplomacy and seemed to refrain from using his station as a herald for the masses or a voice of either solace or guidance during the troubled times. Indeed, even after the war had passed, the pope shunned as much contact with both his clergy and his congregants as was possible given his ceremonial role, enlisting the help of a nun (unofficially dubbed La Popessa) as a sort of private secretary/gatekeeper from both extra-Vatican matters and matters of the Curia itself. He was prone to put off decisions and business matters and, in some views, neglected much of the day-to-day operations of the Church, including such matters as appointments and promotions for reasons as inconsequential as personal whims and grudges held over from his pre-pope days. As a result, the College of Cardinals, upon whom the actual election of a new pope would fall, was grossly understaffed at only fifty-one members.

The election takes place in conclave, whereby the cardinals are quite literally locked within the Vatican palace and kept incommunicado until the papal successor is named. Communication to the outside world is solely through a smoke signal of white or black smoke from the chimney, which keeps everyone outside of the sealed-off Vatican updated on the status of the election. Politicking and extra-Vatican communication are verboten under penalty of ejection.

Once inside it soon became obvious that there was a schism among the cardinals. The liberals had all lined up behind Giacomo Lercaro, the archbishop of Bologna, who favored a simplification of the liturgy and a heavier social involvement on behalf of the Church. The conservatives had originally thought they would be in support of Giovanni Battista Montini, the archbishop of Milan, but Pius had failed to promote him to cardinal by the time of his passing (which some attribute to the old and cranky pontiff's personal splenetic nature), which many in conclave thought rendered him ineligible for election. As a result, the second-choice conservative candidate was Giuseppe Siri, the archbishop of Genoa, who was thought to be even further right than Pius XII, and was, even more to the detriment of his electability, only fifty-two, which many feared might result in another long-term-unto-stagnation papacy since the pontiff, once elected, served unto death.

It soon became clear that neither camp had a majority of votes in their control, and that unless something was done soon, the entire College of Cardinals would be in for a long and highly spartan sojourn in seclusion, a prospect that none of the elder statesmen of the Church relished.

A few of the representatives from the right met with a few of the representatives from the left and hatched a compromise plan. Both realized that neither camp was really prepared for this election, and what was really necessary was a pontiff who would basically put a kind face on the papacy to make up for the aloofness of Pius XII, a kindly old grandfather sort who would allow them to keep the Vatican household in order with the necessary number of appointments and business matters that his predecessor had been stonewalling for way too long. Just as important, they decided that the new pope should already be in his twilight years so that the next election, the one that they would be adequately prepared for, would not be too long in coming.

What the Church really needed was a short interim papacy.

No more, no less.

There had been popes who were little more than place markers in history before. Surely the Almighty would not object to their election of one less divinely inspired pontiff for the sake of the long-term health of the Church.

As a result, Cardinal Angelo Giuseppe Roncalli, the patriarch of Rome, was elected pontiff. He was neither well known nor an intellectual theologian. More important though, he seemed to be well liked by the people of Rome, and most important he was seventy-six years old.

He would be the perfect anti-Pius, a gregarious papal grandfather who could do the necessary glad-handing while appointments were made to pave the way for his successor (most probably Montini, who would now be assured of his cardinalship since he and Roncalli had been friends for quite a long time).

Thus Roncalli ascended to the throne of Saint Peter, whereby he assumed the papacy, taking the name and title of Pope John XXIII.

Contrary to the machinations of Vatican political insiders, the election, in retrospect, seems to have been truly divinely and ever-so-subtly inspired, because the kindly old grandfather pontiff who had been chosen as a placeholder by his mortal contemporaries wound up being one of the most internationally influential pontiffs of the modern age.

More than just putting a new and kinder face on the Church, John succeeded in putting through a series of reforms that quite literally brought the Church into the twentieth century. During his five-year papacy John took the bull by its papal horns and issued numerous encyclicals and divinely inspired pronouncements that angered many of the conservatives who longed for the continuation of the status quo. In particular, his "*Pacem in Terris*" and "*Mater et Magistra*" invoked a deeper understanding of both theological philosophy and the role of the Church in the world today, not just its reverence but its obligation as well.

John also took seriously his title as Bishop of the Diocese of

Rome. His predecessors seemed to have relegated this role to more of an honorary title than an actual appointment, and showed a marked preference toward running all of the papal affairs from the home turf of the Vatican territories. John looked upon the bishopric as an additional responsibility, and indeed an honor that enabled him to maintain a grassroots contact with his flock through frequent parish visitations, including recently incorporated parishes outside of the city limits that were nonetheless part of the diocese of Rome.

Furthermore, John traveled extensively throughout the world, commented on non-Church matters, and even convened a Second Vatican Council to help reform the Church, strive for ecumenism, and indeed open the proverbial Church doors to a more active role for the laity. He convoked the Roman Synod and established the Commission for the Revision of the Code of Canon Law. Many of the prohibitions of the past were relaxed, and the rigidity of Church ritual and dogma (such as the Latin mass) were reformed in a way to make them more parishioner-friendly and relevant to the church-goers of today. Indeed his overall teaching turned the tide of the papal seat from that of an overseer to one of a beacon of hope enlightening the future in hopes of guiding its flock forward.

Though relatively short-lived in terms of papal reigns, John XXIII set a revolution in motion that couldn't be stopped, and when he was succeeded by his old friend Montini (who took the name Paul VI), the objectives of the conservatives had been already skewered, leaving his successor with little choice but to carry out the divinely inspired objectives that John had already set in motion.

As a result, the short interim papacy of the placeholder pope revolutionized the Catholic Church and afforded John XXIII a place on the list of the most influential pontiffs in Church history.

YOU ARE RUNNING AGAINST WHOM?

You often can choose your friends. Sometimes you can pick your ene-mies. Just be careful whom you pick. . . .

PAT BROWN AND THE GOVERNOR'S RACE

CALIFORNIA, 1966

Brian M. Thomsen

Edmund G. "Pat" Brown had entered public life as a district attor-ney, quickly ascended to the position of attorney general and in 1959 became the thirty-second governor of the state of California, with a successful term in office that included a statewide water plan, improvements in higher education, and an advocacy toward the use of computers in state government.

Politically, Democrat Brown was riding high. His advocacy of the liberal agenda and the reinvention of state government coin-cided with the presidential victory of Lyndon Johnson over con-servative Barry Goldwater in 1962. Indeed his own gubernatorial victory over Republican challenger Richard Nixon had cemented his reputation as a political giant killer.

Ever shrewd, Brown realized that his reelection in 1966 might be problematic. The controversial subject of capital punishment had reared its head and his sixty-day reprieve of convicted mur-derer Caryl Chessman (who was nonetheless eventually executed) had caused some division in his base, and the beginnings of widespread unrest on the college campuses was troubling from both a civil peace perspective as well as from a public relations stance given the widespread coverage it was receiving in the national media.

Brown knew that even the giant killer who slew Nixon's chances at the governorship was destined to meet some fierce opposition at the hands of his critics and that his own reelection this time was far from a sure thing.

Worse yet, the favored son of the Republican Party that was slated to run against him had crossover appeal to Brown's own liberal base.

George Christopher, a Greek immigrant at the age of two, had a loyal California following. After a successful career in the dairy business, Christopher began a political career in 1946 by being elected to the San Francisco Board of Supervisors, and in 1955 was elected mayor. Particularly troubling to Brown was that in Christopher's reelection bid in 1959, his opponent had successfully painted him with a liberal paintbrush, claiming that under his mayoralty Christopher had allowed San Francisco to "become the national headquarters of organized homosexuals in the United States."

Here was a Republican challenger who might have more appeal to Brown's base than other Democrats. What Brown needed was a more right-wing Republican opponent than Christopher. But who?

As the Republican primary drew closer, Brown was relieved to find that a more ideal opponent had thrown his hat in the ring, a candidate who could be painted as a right-wing extremist in line with the police-state-loving Republican Party as emblematized by Goldwater and Nixon.

Moreover this opponent was a political neophyte with little to no mainstream practical business experience.

Better yet he was an actor more identified with his role as the shill host for the *Death Valley Days* TV show than as a serious public persona. His recently released autobiography, *Where's the Rest of Me?*, only further denigrated his image with a Hollywood air of superficiality that called to the public mind images of him taking second billing to a chimp and divorcing Jane Wyman, everyone's favorite mother from *Father Knows Best*. Add to that his jingoistic term at the Screen Actors Guild and his naming names back in the era of the Hollywood Ten, and no one would dare ascribe to him any liberal appeal.

Brown was sure that there would be little crossover with his supporters, and given the fact that Democrats greatly outnumbered Republicans in the state voting rolls, victory would be a shoo-in.

But in order for this right-wing neo to get the Republican nomination, he had to win the Republican primary over the sure hand and experience of Christopher, and this was by no means a sure thing.

So Brown decided to help the neophyte along by making statements that would clearly differentiate him from Christopher for the Republican base, casting him as a John Birch extremist rather than the plainspoken everyman that he had played on screen for a very lucrative, non-everyman salary. He even focused the Republican debate on civil rights so that everyone could see that there really was next to no difference between his own views and those of Christopher.

This left the Republican base with a simple conclusion: Why run a candidate who is just a watered-down Democrat?

The plainspoken actor easily beat his seasoned competitor and secured the Republican nomination with a little help from his adversary in the state house.

Brown's plan had worked.

He had secured the opponent of his choosing. He would beat this bad actor, who would then return to the realm of bad television, where he would bore his way through endless cocktail parties of the rich and worthless while the Democrats kept control of the Golden State all to themselves.

Now victory was almost assured . . . but not quite.

On Election Day (November 8, 1966), the giant killer was taken down by his opponent of choice.

Ronald Reagan defeated Brown by a huge majority, taking close to a million votes more than the incumbent mustered. Moreover, Reagan swept all but three of the state's fifty-eight counties, with numbers that amounted to almost the full registered strength of the Republican Party plus almost four hundred thousand Democrat crossover votes.

Brown's plan of picking his opponent had completely backfired. Rather than having to choose between two similar candidates, Brown's choice of Reagan provided voters with an alternative that they quickly supported. In addition to energizing his opposition's base, Brown still lost the support of those in his own party, for whom his handling of troubled issues appeared problematic.

The bad actor had delivered the performance of his life to great applause and luminous reviews.

The viewers/voters liked him so much they demanded a sequel, and the road to the White House was just what the candidate had in mind.

Ronald Reagan distinguished himself as the great communicator and set forth an era of change known as the Reagan Revolution, aimed at reinvigorating the American people with a hefty dose of self-reliance while weaning them off a reliance on government and its publicly funded programs. He worked with Congress to obtain legislation designed to stimulate economic growth, curb inflation, decrease unemployment and strengthen national defense. Indeed his "peace through strength" is credited by many with turning the tide of the Cold War, and bringing about the overall collapse of the Soviet Union as a bellicose world power.

The Ronald Reagan show at 1600 Pennsylvania Avenue was renewed for a second season in 1984 with an electoral landslide unprecedented in modern U.S. elections.

The easier-to-beat candidate chosen by Governor Pat Brown was now proven to be unbeatable—in California, across the country, and in the international political theater. It is entirely possible that he might not have been able to win that Republican primary back in 1966 without a little help from his Democratic opponent, but from that point on he was unstoppable.

Always remember, if given a choice, choose your opponent wisely, not just for the opening sprint, but for the entire race as well, because some people never stop running and before you know it they are so far ahead of the pack, they are just unbeatable.

You Quit What Show?

TV is such a fertile field for finding gross stupidity and highly paid idiots that this section was hardly taxing to write, but it was too much fun for us to resist.

TV LAND: FROM 1970 TO NEXT SEASON

Brian M. Thomsen

Ronnie Schell had gotten himself attached to a really big thing. *Gomer Pyle*, the military life spin-off from *The Andy Griffith Show*, was doing great in the ratings, and his steady role as second banana between Jim Nabors's country-boy Pyle and Frank Sutton's abrasive marine corps sergeant guaranteed him a few audience laughs each week, and, most important, a steady paycheck.

But when he was offered the opportunity to be a headliner for a different show with a role more equal to that of Sutton or Nabors, how could he refuse?

The answer was he couldn't.

So faster than you could say prime time, he resigned from *Gomer Pyle* (really failed to renew his contract, since these negotiations took place during the off-season) to take the lead in the new situation comedy *Good Morning, World,* based around an early morning radio program.

Doing radio on television was a can't-miss concept for laughs. How could it miss?

It did.

Good Morning, World failed to last a season, but lucky for Schell *Gomer Pyle* (now *Gomer Pyle, U.S.M.C.*) welcomed him back, slightly poorer, definitely humbled, but nonetheless grateful.

Ronnie Schell was one of the lucky ones; he had a show that wanted him back.

Others were not so lucky.

McLean Stevenson was riding high. *M*A*S*H* was a huge success with a promising (and as it turned out, long-lived) future ahead of it, and his role of Commanding Officer Henry Blake was a fan favorite and an integral part of the ensemble. But Stevenson wasn't satisfied. Alan Alda and Wayne Rogers got top billing and all of the best lines, and quite frankly he was sick and tired of playing second banana.

He wanted his own show.

So he negotiated his way out of his contract.

Both Henry Blake and McLean Stevenson would leave the M*A*S*H 4077 for greener pastures (well, at least Stevenson would; Blake, the character, never made it home, and was reported missing and presumed dead, thus making a repentant return à la Ronnie Schell extremely unlikely).

In no time at all, Stevenson had his own show, a surefire can't-miss situation comedy with a great new concept. The show's name was *Hello, Larry,* and it was about an early-morning radio show host. After all, a TV sitcom about a radio show was obviously a can't-miss concept (or at least a can't-miss-twice concept).

Hello, Larry failed to last the season and has entered TV history as a certified member of the Hall of Turkeys.

His *M*A*S*H* character having gone down somewhere in the Pacific Ocean, and Stevenson himself having burned a few bridges with the *M*A*S*H* folks, he soldiered on with a new show. The problem with *Hello, Larry* now seemed so obvious: it didn't advertise its biggest selling point. This was rectified with his new series, the strategically titled *The McLean Stevenson Show.*

It, too, sunk like a stone, as did the following year's entry, *In the Beginning* (Stevenson as an old-fashioned priest with Priscilla Lopez as a streetwise nun), which garnered an even smaller audience than its two predecessors, and worse than that proceeded to offend them with its less-than-respectful content. It was yanked off the air before all of its episodes had even been aired.

From that point on Stevenson was on his way to just being a guest on quiz shows and other people's sitcoms, and occasional dinner theater for less-than-demanding audiences who felt bad that his character had been killed on *M*A*S*H.*

Others are guilty of leaving successful shows to pursue bigger and better things, not just their own TV series, but bigger things like major motion pictures—and here too success is never guaranteed, nor is it even the norm. For every John Travolta Academy Award–nominated performance in *Saturday Night Fever*, there is a Bill Murray serious debut in *The Razor's Edge*, and for every Bruce Willis (then of *Moonlighting*) blockbuster breakout in *Die Hard*, there is a Ken Wahl (then of *Wiseguy*) bust out in *The Taking of Beverly Hills.*

Take the case of David Caruso, who had landed various dramatic supporting roles in movies like Sylvester Stallone's blockbuster *First Blood*. His career was going all right, but nobody was really noticing him.

Then along comes a daring new TV series that was out to redefine the words "cutting-edge TV." It was called *NYPD Blue*, and faster than you can say *Dragnet* the show was a hit and Caruso was everyone's favorite TV cover boy. But that wasn't good enough for Caruso. For him, TV was only meant to be a springboard to bigger and better things, so even though the show was a success with a bright and promising future, Caruso said good-bye to prime-time TV to headline such major motion pictures as *Jade* and *Kiss of Death*. Both bombed and bounced him back off the A List until many years later, when he returned to success via TV as he once again pinned on a shield as a TV cop, this time for *CSI: Miami*.

However, bad TV decision making is not restricted to the male of the species.

Shelley Long's Diane Chambers was one of TV's most endearing and irritating characters and her cat-and-dog relationship with Sam Malone (Ted Danson) on *Cheers* was one of the major reasons people tuned in from week to week . . . but it wasn't the only reason, as she found out when her demands became slightly excessive. As a result she decided to leave the success of the show for greener pastures on the silver screen. After an initial success in a buddy film with Bette Midler called *Outrageous Fortune*, Long belly-flopped along in one dreadful comedy after another from *Irreconcilable Differences* to *Troop Beverly Hills* to *Hello Again*.

She was still irritating, but not quite so endearing, and the audiences who tuned in to *Cheers* apparently had been doing so for reasons other than the presence of Shelley Long.

Cheers continued to thrive while Shelley took a long nosedive.

Everyone on this list is among so many highly talented actors and actresses, all of whom just knew that even greater success was just a starring role away, but for whom it wasn't. Who will be missing from your favorite series next fall?

You Forged What?

When you are at the top of your field, well respected and overcoming earlier adversity, what is there left to do? Why, screw it all up entirely, of course.

DAVID BEGELMAN, STUDIO PRESIDENT
HOLLYWOOD, 1976

Robert Greenberger

In Hollywood you have to play along to get along. For the rich and famous and powerful, that was rule number one. For others, though, playing along was never an option.

Take Cliff Robertson for example. An actor best known for the film *Charly*, Robertson was surprised when the IRS went looking for their fair share of the $10,000 Columbia Pictures paid him on September 2, 1976. It said so right there on the 1099 form he received in January 1977. The actor had no idea what they were talking about and he asked his secretary to look into this.

A supervisor at Columbia's accounting department checked Robertson's file and saw the cashed check. He recognized the signature as looking more like studio president David Begelman's than Robertson's.

Robertson's quest took him to Begelman's office, where the veteran show-business executive had issued the check. Begelman told Robertson's accountant that someone in the New York office cut the check and forged the signature. The unfortunate employee had since been sacked and this would not happen again. While the president was hoping that would end it, Robertson began to wonder how someone in the New York office could pull off such a stunt. His further inquiries led to the inevitable conclusion that Begelman himself forged the signature.

Commentator David C. Thompson described Begelman at Salon.com: "Begelman had been a show-business agent, a wheeler-dealer, a charmer, a liar, a gambler, a womanizer, an entertainer, a man who gave big dinners and picked up the tab, and good at all of it. He was widely liked, if not overly trusted."

Normally, people reinvent themselves all the time, but Begelman seemed to make a career out of it, starting with his claim to having graduated from Yale, when the university had no record of his ever attending.

Begelman may have begun his career as an agent at MCA in 1948, but he rose to prominence in 1960 when he and Freddie Fields formed Creative Management Associates. The new talent firm rose in prominence from just four clients (Judy Garland, Polly Bergen, Phil Silvers and Kirk Douglas) to become one of the most powerful institutions in Hollywood.

In 1968 he joined Columbia Pictures as an executive and rose to power as president in 1973. While in the president's office, he oversaw a renaissance that literally saved the financially strapped firm. Hits under his tenure included *The Way We Were, Tommy, Shampoo* and *Close Encounters of the Third Kind.*

It took five months for news of the check forging to reach CEO Alan Hirshfeld. Hirshfeld, Begelman's superior at Columbia, was shocked by the admission of guilt. The news was still contained within the company to a handful of people. Hirshfeld decided to hush the entire thing up rather than fire Begelman outright and expose the company to a public scandal. He suspended his employee for two months, at full pay ($300,000 annually), while the DA continued to investigate. In all, Begelman was found to have embezzled $40,000 from Columbia, including checks to director Martin Ritt and restaurateur Pierre Groleau. Additionally, it was learned the president padded his generous expense account by some $23,000.

It became apparent that Begelman had a gambling problem and needed the cash to cover his bets. The gambling addiction continued for the rest of his life and went untreated.

During this time, Begelman was lobbying for reinstatement, and it came to a head during a board of directors meeting at a corporate retreat that Begelman was invited to, and he had many allies on the board. The agenda was overshadowed with corporate indecision. They asked themselves if it was worth firing a successful executive over what amounted to, in Hollywood's economy, pocket change. While the Board returned Begelman to his job in December, they had also cajoled Robertson into keeping mum. At the time of his reinstatement, the press release referred to Begelman's emotional problems, which were being treated by trained professionals, so no one thought he should lose his job over the indiscretion.

Robertson was pissed. His wife, Dina Merrill, put Robertson in touch with Katharine Graham, the legendary publisher of the *Washington Post*. He gave the first in a series of interviews, shining an unwelcome spotlight on the institution. "There is a spreading cancer of corruption in Hollywood," he told the *Post*, "of which the

Begelman incident is but one example." To the Associated Press, he said, "Wealth and power create a kind of atmosphere of fear. I think they begin to believe that they are above the law."

Additionally, by this point the board also learned of other irregularities, such as the $35,000 charged to *Tommy* for acoustical work. It turns out the work was done by an architect not for the rock opera but for Begelman's home screening room.

Entertainment columnist Liz Smith dubbed the event Hollywoodgate in honor of the recently finished Watergate scandal that forced a president to resign. People couldn't get enough of the story and media outlets were only too happy to provide whatever tidbits they could find.

Ray Stark, a producer who had close ties to Columbia's board, approached Robertson and asked him to keep quiet. He even hinted that Begelman might commit suicide if the pressure was not removed. Robertson remained steadfast in his convictions.

By now there was enough ink devoted to these goings-on that the Securities and Exchange Commission was forced to open their own investigation. Suddenly, the studio was being dragged through the mud, which annoyed stockholders as their stock value dwindled and tarnished Hirshfeld's reputation. It cost them performers who refused to go near the studio. The board had seen enough, and at the July 1978 meeting voted not to renew his contract. It was felt that a clean break was needed for the studio's own good.

David McClintick provided the most sobering coverage in the pages of the *Wall Street Journal*. Lynda Obst, who became a successful Hollywood producer, was editor of the *New York Times*'s Sunday magazine at the time. She first heard about problems with the Columbia board at a cocktail party. She concluded there was an interesting story about the Hollywood–Wall Street connection and hired Lucian K. Truscott IV to write the story under her supervision. Truscott proved to be unreliable, with a history of problems, so the story, which hit on February 26, 1977, caused a stir. Its errors led to threats of lawsuits, and three months later the *Times* printed its lengthiest retraction of all time—at least until 2003 with their own internal scandals. One of Obst's sources was producer Jon Peters, who later went on to run Columbia. When she moved to California, he hired her.

Begelman had little choice but to resign his post, forfeiting $1.25 million in stock warrants. The DA decided to prosecute in 1978 and Begelman pleaded no contest and repaid his former employer the $63,000. His sentence was three years probation, a $50,000 fine and three years of community service. Begelman talked this down to one, which resulted in the anti-drug documentary *Angel Dust*.

During this time, Robertson, for refusing to keep quiet about the check, wound up blacklisted in Hollywood and didn't work for four years. Begelman, though, one of the Hollywood insiders dating back to 1948, was handed an independent production deal with his former studio—the usual parting gift for studio execs.

Begelman shrugged off the scandal and wound up back as president and CEO of MGM/UA. His five-year contract was generous, but his performance was lackluster. The studio lacked major hits outside the James Bond franchise, which was showing signs of age, and Begelman was at a loss. In 1982, during his tenure, McClintick's book about the Hollywood scandal, *Indecent Exposure*, came out and became a best seller. Begelman's woes were on everyone's lips and old problems were reexamined. He settled with the board and once again became an independent producer. This time, he teamed with the Texas billionaire Hunt brothers and entrepreneur Bruce McNall, forming Sherwood Productions. They produced a handful of films, including the cult favorite *The Adventures of Buckaroo Banzai: Across the Eighth Dimension* and the commercial hit *WarGames*.

Begelman and McNall folded Sherwood and replaced it in 1984 with Gladden Entertainment, which had better luck with *Weekend at Bernie's* and *The Fabulous Baker Boys*. Unfortunately, McNall proved to be as unscrupulous as Begelman and forced the company into bankruptcy in 1994 after defaulting on $4.1 million in residuals owed to the various talent guilds. In 1995, McNall was found guilty of receiving bank loans using fraudulent collateral. By this point, Begelman had had enough. On August 7, 1995, he took his own life at the Century Plaza Hotel Towers, leaving no note. His show-biz legacy was forever tarnished by his psychological compulsion to cheat.

The story never went away and Robertson never stopped talking about it. In 1984, he said, "Hollywoodgate is something that has changed the whole industry; it showed that you could confront high-level corruption and still exist. For many years there was an unwritten rule in this town, 'Thou shalt not confront top moguls on corruption or thou shalt not work.' Fifty years from now it won't be my Oscar or anything else I might win that I will be remembered for, but probably this . . . I think there are a few people who wish Hollywoodgate would blow away, just as there are those who wish Watergate will blow away. Neither will."

Begelman's scandalized life remains entombed in McClintick's book, which is still in print. A film version continues to be developed in Hollywood despite speculation it'd never be made since no one wants the spotlight shined on a town built on shady dealings.

Columbia's mishandling of the affair was analyzed in Steven Fink's *Crisis Management: Planning for the Inevitable.*

Robertson went on to resume his active career, as seen in his role as Uncle Ben in 2002's smash success *Spider-Man.*

You Switched Over to What?

If you were not watching the game when this happened, you missed one of life's great frustrations.

NEW YORK/OAKLAND NFL GAME, 1968

Brian M. Thomsen

By the fall of 1968 network executives were aware that television was changing at a dramatic pace, and that the old way of doing things was evolving in a way that required a different sort of decision making on a programming level.

Nowhere was this more evident than at NBC, which had become fearful that one of its long-standing family franchises, essentially "must-see TV" before the sell line was the glimmer of a cliché in some ad exec's mind, might be in jeopardy.

"Walt Disney Presents the Wonderful World of Color," which NBC had taken over from ABC several years earlier in order to lock down family viewership on Sunday nights, was no longer considered a long-term sure thing. The death of host and creative godfather Walt Disney the year before had raised several questions about the ongoing viability of what was essentially an anthology slot of different series programs all aimed at the same audience and developed by the same producer without the essential week-to-week cast consistency that seemed to be driving other shows. The former powerhouses of the anthology genre, such as *Playhouse 90* and *The Twilight Zone*, had all fallen by the wayside and the Disney show without Walt Disney himself might become a problem. As a result, NBC decided to hedge its bets slightly by producing other family entertainment events for the Disney slot in the event that "the Wonderful World of Color" lost its viability. These events would fall under the category of "Specials" and in no way violated their programming agreement with Disney, and would be heavily promoted across the NBC schedule to assure maximum viewer awareness in hopes of expanding the audience for their family programming plans.

A two-hour dramatization of Johanna Spyri's *Heidi* was one such project. Directed by Delbert Mann with TV casting coups of Michael Redgrave, Maximilian Schell, and Walter Slezak (as well as the always popular Jean Simmons and angelic newcomer Jennifer Edwards), and a screenplay by Earl Hamner Jr. (who would later father the family-friendly TV series *The Waltons*), *Heidi* was the type of prestigious family entertainment that NBC wanted to be reflective of its programming. It was promoted heavily in all of the traditional outlets with cover placement for their advertisments in magazines and TV program guides, as well as supported by an extensive outreach program to schools in hopes that students might be encouraged or better yet assigned to watch the program in relation to class work.

All of the early promotion and marketing support came off without a hitch and the buzz on the program was extremely positive, so by the time the airdate of November 17, 1968, rolled around, nothing was left to do but broadcast the much-anticipated film at its designated time slot of 7:00 P.M. EST. This job fell to NBC executive Dick Cline in the New York office.

Dick had his orders and was ready and waiting to make *Heidi* the network success they all wanted.

Unfortunately, there was a situation developing. There was an AFL game slotted prior to 7:00 and a confluence of events began to make it extremely likely that the conclusion of the live broadcast of the game might run beyond 7:00.

Now bear in mind that in 1968 football on TV had not yet achieved its dominance in terms of viewership and the multimillion-dollar broadcast contracts that would arrive with Roone Arledge's maximizing of the game's TV potential. Also the AFL was considered the weak sister to the NFL, and, moreover, the entire operation was considered no better than second string to prime-time programming, let alone the airing of a "Special."

Cline knew what he had to do. The policy was simple: unless otherwise directed, broadcast of the game was to be terminated at 6:59 so that the normal schedule (led off by the heavily promoted *Heidi*) could commence promptly at 7:00.

The game was the New York Jets versus the Oakland Raiders. Both teams had 7–2 records and led their divisions, and both the sports division and the fans were as excited about this televised AFL matchup as they had ever been about an AFL game. Both teams made good on the promise of the situation by playing with great heart and vigor, delivering a satisfying but close game all the way through, so that by the time 6:59 P.M. rolled around with fifty seconds left to play, football fans were on the edge of their seats as the Jets led Oakland by a score of 32 to 29.

Behind the scenes things were a little tense. NBC president Julian Goodman changed his mind and decided to delay the start of *Heidi* by a few minutes so that the telecast of the entire game could be completed. Unfortunately, many viewers were also interested in whether the game or *Heidi* would have preference at 7:00 and decided to call the station. This basically blew out the NBC switchboard, so that no call could get through, including Goodman's, and, as a result, at the designated time, Cline did his duty, switched the switch, and *Heidi* aired.

True football fans, what there were of them, might be disappointed, but with only fifty seconds to go the game was pretty much over anyway.

No harm done . . . right?

Wrong.

To quote the great philosopher Yogi Berra, "it ain't over till it's over," and no better example of this maxim exists than in the outcome of this now-infamous Jets–Raiders game. Not only did Oakland manage to get a touchdown and take the lead, they also returned a fumbled kickoff for a touchdown, securing the Raiders a 43–32 victory over the Jets in less than a minute of play in what has been historically labeled as "the greatest football finish that was never seen."

Football fans roared in righteous indignation, cursing the little Swiss girl who had blocked their viewing of such a great finish, and they let their anger be known.

NBC was shocked.

They never knew they had so many football fans and they were completely taken by surprise at the sudden turn of events.

The *Daily News* headline read, "Jets 32, Raiders 29, Heidi 14."

You Broke In Where?

What really bothers people about this whole thing was how unnecessary it was.

PRESIDENT RICHARD M. NIXON
WASHINGTON, D.C., 1971

Laura Gilman

Richard Nixon was first elected to the House of Representatives in 1947, and held the office of vice president under Dwight Eisenhower for two terms before losing the presidential race to John F. Kennedy in 1960, and then finally won the presidency in 1968. His career, however, will be best remembered for five words: "I am not a crook!" With that statement Richard Milhous Nixon defended himself—ultimately, in vain—on national television against involvement in what came to be known as the Watergate scandal.

Then-president Nixon's guilt can and will doubtless be debated for years to come. What is beyond question, however, is that he was at the center of a scandal that changed how Americans looked at the presidency, transformed how the news media handled the White House, and left an imprint in the political landscape that echoes today when we add "-gate" to the current scandal in the news.

The events that led to Watergate "officially" began in 1971, when the Committee to Re-Elect the President (CREEP, perhaps one of the most unfortunately chosen acronyms in the history of such things) was founded by Nixon's aides. According to later allegations, CREEP existed for the sole purpose of ensuring that Nixon was reelected by any means necessary, including payment (with funds taken from campaign monies) for the illegal surveillance of political opponents, particularly Larry O'Brien, the head of the Democratic National Committee. The means of that surveillance included illegal wiretaps and recordings, and the use of incriminating material to silence critics.

One documented example of the works CREEP funded occurred on September 9, 1971, when a group of men nicknamed "the plumbers" broke into the offices of a Washington psychiatrist in order to find potentially damaging information on Daniel Ellsberg, the man who leaked sensitive information known as the Pentagon Papers—the Defense Department's "secret history" of the Vietnam War—to the press, giving rise to questions about Nixon's handling of the war.

There were other less-than-legal excursions as well, all funded by CREEP, but the scandal really started almost a year later, on June 17, when five men were arrested during an attempted break-in at the Democratic National Committee headquarters in the Watergate Hotel and office complex. It was soon revealed that one of the burglars was James McCord, the security director of CREEP. This connection was the first potentially incriminating link between criminal actions committed on the president's behalf and the president himself.

Two days after the arrests, former attorney general John Mitchell, head of the Nixon reelection campaign, denied that CREEP was in any way connected to the break-in. But the conspiracy was already starting to fall apart. It was discovered that the

DNC headquarters had previously been bugged, and all the threads of evidence pointed toward the Nixon camp.

The Federal Bureau of Investigation eventually traced the money carried by the burglars back to CREEP, at which point Nixon ordered the CIA to call off the investigation, saying that national security was at stake. This, of course, merely heated up the rumors of Nixon's involvement.

At first, the bungled Watergate burglary was shrugged off by most Americans as "just politics," or the maneuverings of particularly overzealous and misguided supporters of the president. However, there were reporters who were not willing to let it rest, and their digging revealed that this was merely the latest in a series of events that could be tied back to CREEP—including the fact that James McCord could be linked to G. Gordon Liddy, general counsel of CREEP, who could in turn be linked to $200,000 in cash that CREEP had given him to fund these "extracurricular" activities. Through this chain, the break-ins were tied directly and irrefutably to Nixon's people, if not the White House itself.

Worse, investigations were soon to reveal that former attorney general John Mitchell had personally approved numerous illegal activities against the 1972 campaign run by Nixon's Democratic opponent, George McGovern. In this tangle of lies, lawbreaking and betrayal of public trust, opinion began to turn against the president, despite his continued denials of wrongdoing.

There is little doubt that these men acted with the knowledge, if not on the orders, of then-president Nixon. The question is, having been elected to one of the most powerful positions in the world, with a high approval rating (at the time of the break-in in 1972, Nixon won reelection by a landslide against challenger

McGovern), why did Nixon and his supporters feel the need to go to such extremes, to not only break the law but to later perjure themselves about it?

To understand what happened, we first need to understand the man at the center of the controversy. To some, Richard Nixon was a canny negotiator, able to stand up to the greatest perceived dangers of the late '60s and early '70s—Communist China and the Soviet Union—and bring them to heel. To others, he was an opportunist, adapting his policies for expediency rather than any strong belief, and to yet others he was a hardheaded conservative, out of touch with the times and refusing to listen to the growing antiwar and civil rights movements, despite his election campaign promise to end the war.

He was likely all of those things, depending on your perspective. Smart, yes. Canny, savvy, egotistical—and above all a survivor. But what he was, unarguably, was one of the greatest paranoids to ever hold elected office.

According to aides, he was convinced that he was under constant attack by "liberals, Democrats, intellectuals, journalists, and the Eastern establishment elite," all of whom were determined to see him fail. Nixon didn't just fear shadow enemies, either—he named names, keeping a list of people he believed to be actively plotting against him called the Opponents List and Political Enemies Project. Handed over to the Senate during the course of investigations, the list included people like actor Paul Newman; Ed Guthman, an editor at the *Los Angeles Times*; and Alexander E. Barkan, national director of A.F.L.-C.I.O.'s committee on Political Education; as well as a number of congressmen and senators who had at one time or another opposed Nixon or supported his rivals.

During his presidency, Nixon ordered recording devices be placed in the Oval Office so that he could keep everything said on record, to "preserve an accurate record of his tenure in office" (*Washington Post*). It may have been to ensure that no one was able to claim he said something he didn't, or to keep records of what other people agreed to, or perhaps, simply, to ensure that he had accurate records when he chose to write his memoirs, as most presidents do. ·

Whatever his reasons, it was a ploy that would backfire on him badly in July 1973, when White House aide Alexander Butterfield revealed the existence of these tapes, which were then subpoenaed by a special prosecutor investigating Watergate, and by the Senate committee.

Nixon refused, claiming executive privilege, which was later refuted by the courts. Ordered to hand over the tapes, Nixon finally did in April 1974, saying "[these] include all the relevant portions of all of the subpoenaed conversations that were recorded, that is, all portions that relate to the question of what I knew about Watergate or the coverup and what I did about it." (Nixon's speech of April 29, 1974).

However, it was soon determined that there was a gap of more than eighteen minutes in the tape of a conversation between Nixon and Haldeman on June 20, 1972. A group of technical experts eventually determined that the gap was the result of five separate manual erasures. In other words, someone had *deliberately* erased selected portions of that conversation before handing them over to the court.

In July 1974, the Supreme Court ordered Nixon to supply all relevant material, including documents and the portions of tapes still missing. When he refused, the House Judiciary Committee voted to impeach Nixon on the grounds of obstruction of justice, abuse of power, and refusal to obey a congressional subpoena. When Nixon finally released the missing material in August 1974, it proved that he had authorized the cover-up of illegal activities committed by CREEP as early as June 23, 1972.

Once that evidence was heard, the end could not be far away. And in fact the Watergate scandal ended officially on August 9, 1974, when Nixon became the first president to resign from office.

It would be wrong to assume, however, that his resignation was at any time a foregone conclusion. It is entirely possible, had CREEP committed these acts and not involved Nixon in the aftermath, that the illegalities would have indeed fallen under the heading of "politics as usual." It should not be assumed that politics before this moment had been innocent of such maneuvers, and the phrase "plausible deniability" was created for just such instances. Two actions, however, took the scandal from dirty pool to nation-rocking scandal:

1. Nixon's firm belief that people were out to "get him" both personally and politically, which created an environment in which CREEP seemed like a good idea.

2. The fact that Nixon not only made tapes of his conversations but held on to them even when their destruction would have left the federal investigation without a smoking gun to prove his involvement.

Had Nixon refused to sign off on the cover-up in 1972, or if he had been willing to destroy the tapes, he might have escaped the eventual results. However, he seemed convinced that he would, in the end, be vindicated and his enemies cast down. In light of that, once CREEP's actions were set in motion, the decision to cover up those actions was perhaps inevitable. Ironically enough, it seems that the paranoia that defined him was also what sealed his fate.

You Taped It All?

Rarely is there a case where it is as clearly demonstrated as this one where ego interfered with good sense.

WATERGATE REDUX

WASHINGTON, D.C., 1974

Brian M. Thomsen

There is a sage old bit of legal advice: "Just answer the question directly and succinctly. No more, no less. Don't give the prosecution any reason to say that you are not cooperating, nor tell them any information that they don't already know."

Unfortunately no one seemed to have shared these words of wisdom with former Nixon White House senior aide Alexander Butterfield, whose major task in the administration was to ensure that the president's day ran smoothly.

The Senate select committee investigating the Watergate matter was looking to corroborate some of the testimony given by John Dean, who had mentioned that he might have been taped during some of his conversations with the president. This made perfect sense given the security consciousness of presidential staff members Haldeman and Ehrlichman, and the notion of recording conversations was easily ascribed to some of the cloak-and-dagger plots that were being alleged about the White House.

The matter of inquiry was simple—were the conversations taped?

The answer was equally simple—yes.

The inquisitors, however, never realized that there was more to the answer . . . and it was provided to them on a silver platter.

On July 16, 1973, before the Ervin Committee, Alexander Butterfield acknowledged that indeed there was a taping system in the Oval Office (ergo Dean could have been right and might have been taped).

The question was answered.

The allegation was corroborated.

But Butterfield didn't stop there.

"Everything was taped," he added with no prodding, "as long as the President was in attendance. There was not so much as a hint that something should not be taped."

All the committee had wanted was corroboration.

What they got was a vast resource of potentially incriminating evidence that they did not previously know existed.

If all of the president's conversations were taped, all they needed to do was to review the tapes to see who said what to whom on what day for an accurate record of what really happened. The later revelation that the system was automatically voice-activated further enhanced their value as an accurate record of the conversations since there was no excuse of human error interfering with the record.

The subsequent battle over the release of the tapes by the White House went all the way to the Supreme Court.

The White House lost.

When the first tapes (less than forty hours' worth) were released in April 1974, the pattern of White House action and conversation revealed was enough to provide a framework for the proof of the allegations of abuse of power and obstruction of justice.

The outcome was from that point inevitable.

The president resigned, not over the charge of masterminding a second-rate burglary or violation of civil rights or even lying to the American people, but for failing to sufficiently cover up a cover-up that was unnecessary in the first place.

It was not enough that Butterfield admitted that Dean's conversations were taped. By exposing the existence of the entire taping system, information he inadvertently volunteered, he had laid the groundwork for the impeachment case to come, providing a road map that even a congressional committee would be able to follow.

YOU VACCINATED WHOM
AGAINST WHAT?

The best of intentions, the worst of science. Who says science and politics don't mix? Well, this does.

THE CENTERS FOR DISEASE CONTROL
UNITED STATES, 1976

E. J. Neiburger

The great flu epidemic of 1917–1918 was one of the world's greatest plagues and depopulators of the world. An estimated 20 million to 50 million people died in this great epidemic, though undoubtedly many more folk silently died in uncounted rural settings where public health officials would not visit. Hundreds of millions of people were made ill and never fully recovered. Many, weakened by the flu, became infected with TB, contributing to the future TB epidemics of the 1920s and early '30s, where in many cities one out of every four inhabitants died from "consumption." This influenza epidemic was unique. It came in two waves and killed primarily healthy adults rather than the old, young and feeble, as is usually seen in the commonly experienced annual influenza outbreaks. The 1918 flu was very rapid in its effects, often striking a healthy man in the morning and leaving him dead in the evening. Besides killing humans, this flu subtype also infected and killed pigs.

Over 600,000 Americans died of this rapidly transmitted, air-borne form of Influenza A. Most families affected were isolated by neighbors. Everyone kept to themselves, wore masks and avoided crowds. All economic activity, not to mention World War I, slowed due to disruptions in trade and loss of key personnel. Production of goods and services faltered. The world economy, plagued by end-of-war disruptions, began to fail. In 1976, it looked to some Public Health officials like the 1918 Flu was back. It was a false alarm, but thousands would die in the series of errors that tried to deal with the epidemic that wasn't.

In January 1976, an army private at Fort Dix, New Jersey, reported for sick call. The base physician, Colonel J. Bartley, diagnosed the soldier's illness as an upper respiratory infection and ordered him to rest. Ignoring doctor's orders, the private participated in a late-night march, collapsed and later died at the base hospital. A few hours later, dozens of soldiers reported sick with symptoms of upper respiratory infections.

The base doctors suspected the annual, and normally rather mild, flu, which often affects the population in the winter. They found it in throat swabs of the sick soldiers, but there was also evidence of another unknown virus. The samples were sent to the U.S. Centers for Disease Control (CDC) in Atlanta.

The CDC is the main center for investigative public health in the United States. As a division of the U.S. Department of Health, it was equipped with the "best" scientists and laboratories for detecting diseases and epidemics. It was also considered by many people as a political organization which, at that time, was poorly run, underfunded and relatively dysfunctional. There was a great pressure to find newsworthy epidemics and disease outbreaks in order to justify the CDC's existence. Politics often got in the way of good medicine and science. In fact, a few years earlier, President Nixon had suggested the CDC be closed down because of the inefficiency and politics that were so heavily entrenched.

After receiving the virus samples, the CDC quickly identified the mysterious Fort Dix virus as the 1918 flu virus (Influenza A) and, because of its association with hogs, named it Swine Flu. The CDC urged the Federal Drug Administration (FDA) to publish an official warning that contagious Swine Flu was hiding in the nation's hogs. "Killer pigs" was one byword. Once the media found out (as intended), there was a great public response, which financially allowed the CDC to activate its investigative departments. On February 20, 1976, the CDC started searching the nation's hospitals for Swine Flu patients. They also convened the CDC Advisory Committee on Immunization Practices, which advised the CDC on what actions to take on this matter.

The advisory committee recommended that Swine Flu vaccine be manufactured and stockpiled, and a plan for mass vaccination be created. No other actions were recommended pending future reports of the spread of the "epidemic." CDC leader Dr. David Sencer disregarded the committee's recommendations and sent an Action Memo to the government threatening dire consequences if immediate action was not taken. The CDC (Sencer) recommended an immediate major immunization program. "Better to spend money than to have deaths" was the watchword. Money and authority poured into the previously ignored and cash-strapped CDC.

On March 24, 1976, President Ford made an emergency TV

telecast urging all Americans to have the vaccination. The estimated cost for this program was $135 million. This unusual action was due in part to the threat of an epidemic (as hyped by the CDC) and the need to show "action" in the coming election, which would eventually put Jimmy Carter into the presidency. The only problem, which most people forgot, was that other than a few dozen Fort Dix solders affected in the initial outbreak, no one since had come down with Swine Flu . . . nationwide.

Disaster 1

The National Influenza Immunization Program (NIIP) was a failure nearing disaster. It started three months late. The CDC gave one of the four vaccine manufacturers the incorrect virus to make into vaccine and 2 million doses of the wrong vaccine were produced. Physicians found that the vaccine caused life-threatening side effects in 2 percent of the population. These included fatal anaphylaxis, high fevers (100-plus degrees), headaches, malaise, soreness and a tenfold increase in the crippling Guillain-Barré syndrome. If the vaccine was distributed to the 175 million Americans, hospitals would not be able to cope with the 3 million to 3.5 million immediate illnesses caused by these reactions.

These excessive reactions caused all the vaccine makers to drop the program because of liability. It was estimated that malpractice and product liability litigation would cost the manufacturers $5 billion. The government would have to cover these costs if the program was to continue. It was getting too expensive.

By July 1976, the NIIP was in full swing. Five months passed with only six deaths reported (the original Fort Dix soldiers). Five hundred other soldiers showed increased antibodies to Swine Flu (implying that they were infected), but there was no illness. This was not the typical reaction one would expect from the mass killer Influenza A of 1918. There were no other reports of Swine Flu nationwide. There was no epidemic. There never was. The CDC refused to either accept this fact or admit it was wrong. It continued to go ahead with the NIIP. There was too much money, fame and power at stake. The program was becoming increasingly expensive. Congress was resisting requests for more funding, and because of the lack of victims of this "widespread" epidemic, the program was in danger of being shut down. The folly was obvious to all. The CDC needed an epidemic. They needed bodies in the streets.

Disaster 2: Rescue

It was a terrible time for the CDC. No one was dying from a disease it predicted but had last seen half a century ago. Fortunately for the CDC, between July 27 and August 6, 1976, Pennsylvania physicians noticed an outbreak of a new flu. It had the typical flu symptoms of malaise, muscle aches, critically high fever, headaches and an initial nonproductive cough. Unlike the flu of 1918, it generally infected older people who had existing lung disease and enlarged hearts. First reports came from the Bellevue Stratford Hotel in Pennsylvania, where 10,000 American Legionnaires were meeting at a state convention. Twenty-nine people died and 147 attendees were hospitalized from this strange disease with flulike symptoms. Was it Swine Flu, a commie plot, a new bacterial disease (later called Legionnaires' disease)? No one could immediately say.

The CDC announced the "outbreak *could* be Swine Flu." The symptoms were similar and homebound conventioneers might be

spreading the disease throughout the nation. There was an immediate panic. The media went crazy. Gloom and doom was televised
hourly. Everyone was scared. Resistance to the NIIP program evap-
orated in Congress.

In response to this panic, Congress passed the National Swine Flu
Immunization Program of 1976. This rigid, new program gave the
CDC and FDA money and authority to continue the immunization
program. Two hundred million doses of vaccine were produced.
Eventually 40 percent of the U.S. population was vaccinated. As a
convenience measure, Swine Flu vaccine was mixed with most of the
nation's Victoria Flu (1976–77 annual mild flu) vaccine supply.

There was a problem. By August 20, there were no new cases of
what was termed Legionnaires' disease. There was no evidence of
Swine Flu in these patients or in tests conducted elsewhere in the
United States. The CDC was stumped. On December 6, 1976, three
patients died of side effects a few hours after getting their Swine
Flu shots at a Pittsburgh center. The media picked up this news
and within a month the program was halted. It was obvious: You
had a greater chance of dying from the vaccine than the disease.

Many CDC officials "retired" along with the Ford administration (election loss). The CDC lost authority and funds. The results
of this fiasco were that between 52 and 100 people died directly
from vaccine side effects, and between 600 (official) and 3,675
(nonofficial) were paralyzed with Guillain-Barré syndrome. The
federal government paid billions of dollars to victims and their
families in liability lawsuits. The mixed Victoria–Swine Flu vaccine
was dumped, leaving many elderly citizens without any flu protection for 1976 and 1977. There was not enough time to make new
batches. Thousands of old and immunocompromised patients

died of annual flu. The government proved that it could mount a nationwide vaccine program and vaccinate a significant portion of the population (wrong disease and vaccines were a "minor" issue).

As a representative from the World Health Organization (Dr. G. Nossel) mused, "You Americans ought to have your heads examined . . . No way would we permit it . . . There has been no proper investigation . . . The vaccine has not been properly researched . . . There are too many unknowns."

So ended the great epidemic that wasn't. The CDC, demoralized, shamed and short on funding, wandered through the next four years looking for a new epidemic. In 1981 they hit the jackpot: AIDS. It was time for business as usual.

YOU ARE RESCUING THEM HOW?

A camel is a horse designed by a committee. This was a military action that suffered a similar fate.

PRESIDENT JIMMY CARTER

IRAN, 1979

Robert Greenberger

Jimmy Carter's first term as president was not going well. He accused the country of suffering a malaise as the economy was just beginning to show signs of life after years of turmoil sparked by oil shortages. In fact, oil was very much on his mind throughout the term, winding down in 1979. Carter's intense foreign affairs efforts were focused on bringing peace to the Middle East, culminating in the historic 1977 meeting between Israel's Menachem Begin and Egypt's Anwar Sadat. His diplomacy was widely praised, even though it angered many in the region who harbored deep hatred for the Israelis and their supporters.

In 1979, America was shocked to learn that over sixty hostages were taken when Iranian militants suddenly stormed the embassy in Tehran. Protests against America were nothing new, but the vehemence and frequency of these events had increased under the spiritual leadership of Ayatollah Ruhollah Khomeini, who earlier in the year had returned to his native land from exile.

His return was made possible by the absence of the shah,

Mohammed Reza Pahlavi, who began his rule in 1941. Anger toward America started developing in 1953 when the shah sought U.S. support halting the nationalization of Iran's oil business. In return, America supplied the shah with dollars and military aid, something that lasted from President Eisenhower through Carter.

Secure in his position, a decade later the shah announced social and economic reforms but refused to grant broad political freedom. Nationalists objected to such "Westernizing" of their homeland and riots broke out in 1963. Some of those leaders, including Ayatollah Khomeini, were arrested and deported from their own country.

As the country beefed up its military and continued to do business with the Western powers, the support of the people was eroded. In December 1977, President Carter toasted the shah at a state dinner in Tehran, calling him "an island of stability" in the troubled Middle East. He glossed over the growing number of reports about the people's frustration with their leader. Finally, the citizenry revolted and on January 16, 1979, the shah fled. America refused him entry, so the shah settled in Egypt. A month later, Khomeini triumphantly returned and the volume of protests against America was raised. He gained further influence by refusing to join the new government being formed, seeming to respond more to the people's will.

The final straw for many was when the shah, suffering from cancer, came to America on October 22 for treatment. Khomeini used that to whip his people into a frenzy, and the embassy was assaulted just weeks later.

Carter was reluctant to let the shah fly to America for fear of exacerbating a tense situation. "He went around the room, and most of us said, 'Let him in,'" Vice President Walter Mondale said sometime later. "And he said, 'And if [the Iranians] take our employees in our embassy hostage, then what would be your advice?' And the room just fell dead. No one had an answer to that. Turns out, we never did." A short time later, the radical students in Tehran rioted, stormed the embassy and the "if" came true.

Carter knew enough to ask the question since months before Iranians briefly held the U.S. ambassador hostage until Khomeini insisted he be freed.

Never before had so many citizens been held hostage in a foreign land under peacetime conditions. Nor was it even certain that the new government in Iran had control of the radical students holding the embassy staff. Carter vowed on television that the hostages would be freed and America would not bow to such dangerous zealots. The students who stormed the embassy insisted that America return the shah to them for justice and send a few billion dollars, too. They believed the shah had stolen this money from the people but had no evidence.

Carter needed to shake off the malaise he accused his fellow countrymen of operating under and act. He recognized this could be a defining moment of his first term, and with the election season beginning three months later his every move would be criticized by the Republicans. With that in mind, he immediately embargoed oil from Iran and took the stance that economic sanctions would squeeze the country. On the world stage, Iran was condemned and many countries joined in on the sanctions. Assets were frozen in banks around the globe and the pressure was on.

Within hours, on November 5, the newly certified U.S. Army Special Forces Operational Detachment-Delta (Airborne) was on full alert and plans were being drawn up for a rescue. Colonel Charles Beckwith was the man in command and he immediately saw the complications. Tehran was landlocked, not near any airports, and U.S. intelligence information within the country was scarce and unreliable. With the world spotlight on Washington, it also meant operating in secret, making things much more difficult.

Khomeini, playing to the same world stage, agreed six days later to free female, African-American, and non–U.S. citizen hostages. After that, fifty-three people remained, including, as it turned out, two women and one African American.

Penelope Laingen, wife of hostage Bruce Laingen, chargé d'affaires of the embassy, tied a yellow ribbon around a tree at her Maryland home that December. Her gesture captured Americans' imaginations and millions followed her lead.

And as 1979 became 1980, things remained at a standstill. America refused the demands and tightened the fiscal screws. Khomeini's followers continued the protests, refusing to let anyone else go free.

At first, Carter was praised for being a calm leader, but as winter turned to spring, people were getting tired of the statesman. Caucuses and early primaries were being held and the spotlight never left Iran. People wanted their president to do something beyond speeches. Hawks in Congress wanted a military approach from the outset, but Carter preferred diplomacy. Despite that public stance, the Pentagon had long before begun work on just such a plan. Finally, after months of haggling and delay, on April 11, Carter approved Operation Eagle Claw, sending in troops to free the hostages.

Dr. Zbigniew Brzezinski, the assistant to the president for national security affairs, led the White House group in favor of military action. Secretary of State Cyrus Vance disagreed and ultimately resigned his post. Brzezinski saw this as America's own version of the successful hostage rescue raids at Mogadishu and Entebbe. Delta Force commander Beckwith disagreed, saying, "Logistically speaking it would be a bear. There were the vast distances, nearly 1,000 miles, of Iranian wasteland that had to be crossed, then the assault itself, against a heavily guarded building complex stuck in the middle of a city of 4,000,000 hostile folks. This was not going to be any Entebbe or Mogadishu. Nothing could be more difficult."

Beckwith did approve a plan that called for eight helicopters (USMC RH-53s), twelve planes (four MC-130s for refueling, three EC-130s, three AC-130s, and two C-141s), and numerous operators placed within Tehran ahead of the actual assault. In the days prior to the mission, which was to be based out of Wadi Kena in Egypt, the various vehicles required for the mission were in use, creating an "operational footprint." This would help allay suspicion that the military was on the move.

Training, involving all four branches of the armed services, had begun the previous fall and lasted for 172 days before Carter approved the plan. Obstacles along the way included finding a practical refueling system, which ultimately relied on an older system that had been abandoned. The various aircrews had practiced using the Night Observation Goggles (NOG), still in its infancy. The first MH-53 navy pilots were replaced since they were slow to adapt to the NOGs, but also given their inferior flying tactics. Given their more aggressive approach to flying, marine corp pilots were selected to fly the insertion parts of the mission. Air force pilots served as backup crews, navigating and en route flying.

Like the refueling solution, a notion dating back to the days of the Office of Strategic Services (forerunner to today's CIA) was employed, using a special dark paper to cover the landing lights. This blunted the visible light but allowed infrared emissions through, allowing the NOGs to help them land.

A CIA Twin Otter flew into Iran in March, landing at a spot marked Desert One, with an operative planting landing lights to help guide the forces. It was noted that at 3,000 feet radar was detected but nothing below that altitude. They could land unseen.

On the first night, the plan was to have three MC-130s fly to a barren spot in Iran and offload the Delta Force men, combat controllers, and translators and truck drivers. Three EC-130s would then land and prepare to refuel the marine RH-53s flying in from the U.S. carrier *Nimitz*. Once refueled, the choppers would fly the task force to a spot near Tehran and meet up with the in-country agents, who would lead the operators to a safe house to await the assault the next night. All this flying would be accomplished by "weaving" carefully in between radar tower nodes. The second night would have the MC-130s and EC-130s fly once more into Iran, with one hundred Rangers, headed for Manzariyeh Airfield, which had been built by the shah as a viewing stand for air shows and had therefore been abandoned during his exile. The Rangers would attack while the C-141s would land and transport the hostages back to safe soil.

Nothing went as planned.

On the evening of April 24, the six C-130s left Masirah Island, Oman, and eight RH-53D helicopters departed the USS *Nimitz* in the Arabian Sea.

Two of the helicopters, flying below two hundred feet to be safe from detection, got caught in sandstorms and had to land, as did a third when its warning light went on. Later they described the experience as "flying in a bowl of milk." Collecting the crew from the third helicopter meant the plane was now twenty minutes behind the formation.

The remaining helicopters continued toward Desert One. Word was relayed that the planes and fuel had landed safely so the two grounded choppers lifted off and proceeded to the rendezvous. Yet another helicopter, though, developed a malfunction, grounding it. That left six choppers, the minimum allowed in the plan. Three of the helicopters arrived an hour behind schedule, with the final three turning up seventy-five minutes late. One of them had developed a hydraulic system failure, forcing the mission to be aborted since they were below the operational minimum of six helicopters.

If that wasn't bad enough, after the abort was called one of the helicopters drifted toward a parked plane, intending to refuel. The pilot couldn't see the plane since his rotors kicked up so much sand that visibility was dangerously reduced. The helicopter and plane collided, both going up in flames. Orders were given to evacuate the men, destroy the helicopters and leave the country. While wounded men were removed from the area, the helicopters were never destroyed. Despite their best rescue efforts, five members of the air force and three marines perished. The dead and $193 million in equipment were abandoned.

The following day, Iranian soldiers investigated the crash site and found the vehicles, still intact. They recovered the secret U.S. plans, which nearly cost the Delta operatives their lives. Additionally, the students split the hostages up, preventing future attempts. Khomeini's people crowed about their success against America's highly vaunted army, and in retrospect that failure ended Carter's hopes for a second term.

What went wrong? First an anguished president asked that question, then the public and finally Congress, with extensive hearings.

Studying the failure, the Pentagon learned they were insufficiently prepared despite nearly six months of training. The weather information was inaccurate; the estimate of a twenty-minute flight was off by five hours; and it was learned that many of the marine pilots lacked the skills necessary to complete the mission. In one case, unfamiliarity with the aircraft caused one pilot to ground the aircraft when it could have flown.

The six-member commission headed by Admiral James L. Holloway III explored every step taken, including the selection of aircrew. Navy and marine pilots with little experience in long-range overland navigation or refueling from C-130s were selected, even though more than one hundred qualified air force H-53 pilots were available. It was also determined that the four forces did not train in concert but rather separately, leading to miscommunication during the actual op. Additionally, the panel faulted the decision to use just eight helicopters, just two over the minimum required. Instead, the commission concluded that at least ten and perhaps as many as twelve helicopters should have been used. In review, it was also determined that in-air refueling, rather than hopscotching across the desert, would have been more efficient. It certainly would have avoided the Desert One collision.

Beckwith commented in review, "The assault plan was sketchy. Its chances for success were very slender indeed. The basic scenario looked very complicated. It also revealed that at this time the Armed Forces of the United States had neither the present resources nor the present capabilities to pull it off. Training was needed to accomplish unique and demanding tasks."

In early July, the Iranians released hostage Richard Queen, who had developed multiple sclerosis. It was the only positive step taken by the captors during the year. In America, however, yellow ribbons in support of the remaining fifty-two Americans were seemingly tied around every tree in the country. A newfound sense of patriotism filled the airwaves and people sought out information. ABC responded with a late-night summary of the day's international events that evolved into *Nightline*, still broadcast today with host Ted Koppel.

The shah also died that month, but that seemed to have little effect on either the Americans or the Iranians.

September saw Khomeini saying enough was enough, their point had been made. Mighty America had been humbled and now it was time to release the hostages. Carter personally got involved with the negotiations, distracting him from the brutal election season. The students initially demanded $24 billion from the frozen assets.

On September 22, Iraq invaded Iran, sparking a long simmering war that served to slow down the negotiations, much to Carter's frustration.

Delays, most of which were captured by news crews, hampered the president's effort up to and after he lost in a landslide to Ronald Reagan. He was seen on the phone to Iran even during the January 1981 inauguration. The final deal saw $8 billion in assets unfrozen and a promise to lift the trade sanctions.

Minutes after Reagan was sworn in, the hostages were freed, giving rise to speculation the Republicans were cutting deals behind Carter's back. These allegations were never proven but still haunt the matter.

After 444 days in captivity, the fifty-two hostages flew out of Tehran to the Wiesbaden Air Force Base in West Germany. Reagan wisely asked the former president to be his representative in Germany a day later when the hostages were returned once more to free soil.

Khomeini remained in power until his death years later. His anti-American vehemence became his epitaph. None of the hostages were killed or even abused by the students. The toll of losses was simply eight soldiers in a botched rescue attempt and one president.

You Assassinated Whom?

When you are a revolutionary, it pays to remember who your friends are. The consequences of forgetting can be disastrous.

THE PROVISIONAL IRA

DONEGAL BAY, IRELAND, 1979

Brian M. Thomsen

On August 27, 1979 a kindly old elder statesman of the Crown, his daughter and her husband, their two sons, his dowager mother, and a young (fifteen) aide were enjoying a holiday cruise on Donegal Bay on Ireland's northwest coast on the statesman's twenty-seven-foot fishing vessel, *Shadow V.*

A relaxing and revitalizing time was planned for all, far from the metropolitan mayhem of the cities and the rigors of court and Parliament . . . but such was not to be.

The holiday outing turned into a "political statement" when a fifty-pound radio-controlled bomb was detonated on board, killing the grandfather, one of his grandsons, the aide, and the dowager.

A few hours later the following statement from the Provisional wing of the Irish Republican Army in Belfast was issued: "The IRA claim responsibility for the execution of Lord Louis Mountbatten. This operation is one of the discriminate ways we can bring to the attention of the English people the continuing occupation of our country."

* * *

Lord Louis Mountbatten was an anomaly for the royal family. In addition to being Queen Elizabeth's cousin and the mentor to Prince Charles—Elizabeth's son and heir to the throne of England—Lord Mountbatten was an honest-to-god "war hero" who served with distinction in World War II, including a stint as commander of the British destroyer HMS *Kelly* which was torpedoed several times (and immortalized by Noel Coward in the 1942 classic *In Which We Serve*), after which he continued service in Southeast Asia from 1943 to 1946.

After the war he was named viceroy of India, where he witnessed firsthand the strife and violence that went hand in hand with the handover of power to the Congress Party and the subsequent partition of the Indian subcontinent into separate Muslim and Hindu states.

To say that he was acquainted with unrest caused by religious tensions and political strife in an occupied land is a major understatement.

In addition to his actual service to England, Mountbatten was separated from other members of the royal family for another reason—he was almost universally well liked, and cheered by members of all of England's vastly stratified social classes. Indeed, he also had a soft spot in his heart for Ireland and the Irish people, and since the early seventies had often vacationed there, ignoring the numerous security warnings that had become de rigueur for the entire royal family as a direct result of the so-called troubles pertaining to Northern Ireland.

For some, the murder/bomb plot was seen as a landmark event in the grand scheme of IRA military strategy, but the results were far less earth-shattering. Indeed, in the words of historians Simon

Freeman and Ronald Payne: "The murder changed nothing in the province and only demonstrated, as if it was necessary, that determined terrorists often find ways to murder their chosen targets."

Experts on such matters believed that the plot was really just bait, that is, a reason given to the Crown to reinstitute the sort of harsh security measures that tended to sway Irish public opinion toward the "downtrodden and overmatched revolutionaries" that the IRA positioned themselves as and away from the fascistic establishment of the military and police factions of the British government. Margaret Thatcher, the so-called Iron Lady, had just taken office as prime minister and was expected to take a very hard line on dealing with the disciples of Irish republicanism. The engineers of the bomb plot were sure that this would provide the excuse, but the prime minister failed to take the bait. Ever cautious, she concentrated her initial efforts, marshaling cooperation and coordination on interservice intelligence operations with an accent on the acquisition of information for prevention of future "terrorists' acts" rather than on the type of public-animosity-inducing security crackdown that the plotters had anticipated.

Thus on a simple strategic level, the IRA plot had failed to achieve its desired outcome.

However this was not the only "downside" the plotters experienced.

Irish and British citizens alike were horrified at the choice of Lord Mountbatten as a target. In addition to his service to all British subjects, and his popularity, the former Supreme Allied Commander was viewed by many as being sympathetic toward if not actually supportive of Irish independence, given his own fondness for the land and its people, as well as his own experience as a firsthand witness to the terrible strife that went on during his term as viceroy in India. Here was a voice within the queen's court that might have tempered the expected fire and vitriol from the Iron Lady prime minister, as well as the mind of a skilled politician and diplomat who might have played an instrumental role in a conciliatory truce like the one that was not to occur until twenty years later.

It would appear that the plotters had indeed damaged their own cause in the long term by their choice of targets. They had also earned some of the Crown's portrayal as bloodthirsty murderers and terrorists, and had lost a possible ally to achieve their own alleged goal (namely, independence and peace for all of Ireland), and all for the sake of making a statement that was totally unnecessary and, from a pragmatic point, completely inconsequential.

YOU MADE WHAT?

Okay, more Hollywood. All that money, so much stupidity, so little common sense. We just couldn't resist.

HOLLYWOOD, 1980S–'90S

Brian M. Thomsen

In his insightful masterwork on Hollywood filmmaking, Academy Award–winning screenwriter William Goldman accurately contends that the one basic rule of the screen trade is that "nobody knows nothing."

Multimillion-dollar turkeys are green-lighted every day while executives live with the realization that they are only as secure as their next blockbuster. As a result, the real game in Hollywood is not to discover the next groundbreaking talent, the new Hitchcock or Kurosawa whose films will be studied for centuries to come but rather to latch on to the next sure thing.

Nothing succeeds like success, and the safest decision is usually to stick with what has worked before. Ergo the smart movie mogul will always back a sure thing whether it is a sequel to a blockbuster, a long-awaited collaboration between two popular box-office heavyweights, or even the rare ultracommercial high concept.

Ponder the following sure-to-succeed high concepts:

"What the man who revolutionized the science fiction genre

did with his mega-million blockbuster *Star Wars* (or *Alien*), he now does for fantasy!"

"A madcap big-budget comedy about World War II from the man behind the Indiana Jones films!"

"A hip and now film that does for new wave what *Saturday Night Fever* did for disco!"

"The bestselling master of horror in his directorial debut!"

"America's first lady of comedy in the film version of one of Broadway's top moneymaking musicals of all time!"

"Hepburn and Wayne together for the first time in the sequel to *his* Academy Award–winning performance!"

These are the kinds of films that studio marketing types would like us to believe can literally sell themselves, and that is quite true . . . until someone in the public actually sees one and realizes that the film either doesn't live up to the hype/expectation, or even worse decides that it wasn't a particularly good idea to begin with, despite the hype.

As a result all of the "sure-to-succeed" concepts (including, but not limited to *Willow*, *Legend*, *1941*, *Times Square*, *Maximum Overdrive*, *Mame*, *Rooster Cogburn*, and *Gigli*) failed to succeed.

Maybe someone should have realized that fantasy and science fiction were apples and oranges, or that some ideas weren't either funny or commercial, or that even the most talented of writers might be ill-qualified to handle a film version of his own work, or that class concepts starring seasoned veterans might just wind up being dismissed as dated and possessing limited appeal for the largest segment of the moviegoing public.

The list is almost endless:

- *Howard the Duck* (well, *Superman* worked on film, and besides it's a George Lucas project)

- *The Bonfire of the Vanities* (a multi-week *New York Times* number-one bestseller with Academy Award nominees Tom Hanks and Melanie Griffith, and the Mr. Box Office Blockbuster of the moment, Bruce Willis)
- *MacArthur* (just like the one of Patton, but in the Pacific theater)

Why did we ever think that these would be great films?

Maybe because we were told that they were going to be great.

Why did *they*, the Hollywood power brokers, believe that they would be great films?

In the words of William Goldman, because in Hollywood "nobody knows nothing!" Everybody talks a good line, but when the similes and metaphors and the blandishments and balderdash are all stripped away, it all comes down to a roll of the dice.

There are no sure things, and when it comes to green-lighting a project, it would appear that some studio executives are more motivated by fear of losing a project to the competition than of actually losing money.

No one ever wants to lose the next big thing.

Thus when Michael Cimino pitched his next project after having achieved the status of sophomore wunderkind with the critical and commercial success of *The Deer Hunter*, no one wanted to say no.

Here was a fresh new talent ("there weren't many of them," "who knows when the next one will come along," "he'll still be cheaper and more responsive than someone with a more established reputation"). Here was a high concept—the Johnson County War, the West as it really was ("he can do for cowboys what he did for Vietnam vets," "*The Wild Bunch* worked, it'll probably be like that," "we can't lose!"). It had blockbuster written all over it.

So they gave the man his money and sat back and waited for the final cut . . . and waited . . . and waited.

No one questioned the fact that a leading lady had been cast that no one had ever heard of, or that certain parts required subtitles, or that other parts had their shooting locations switched from New England to England, or that the budget kept getting revised upward.

The man was obviously a genius; there was no reason to doubt him. He even let them see snippets of the work in progress, like the four hours of footage on the film's key battle scene.

He obviously knew what he was doing.

They just kept writing the checks until the film was delivered, late, and very, very long (over three hours).

No problem, they thought, he'll just have to cut it, and fast.

The director wasn't happy. He wasn't used to being told what to do.

But eventually they compromised, and the film was released. Its name was *Heaven's Gate,* and it bankrupted the studio. It was yanked from release in less than a week and was at the time considered to be the costliest bomb/turkey/fiasco of all time.

No big box office.

No Academy Awards.

No nothing, just a ton of red ink and a handful of out-of-work movie executives who couldn't say no.

Predictably a shorter, "more commercial" cut of the film was released a few months later (to try to recoup some of the losses)— it bombed.

Less predictably, a close to four-hour-long director's cut was eventually released on videotape. It actually garnered some nice reviews (maybe because the plot was no longer seen as disjointed as it was in the shorter version).

Maybe if the director had stuck to his guns and forced them to release the longer version, or maybe if the executives had kept a tighter rein on the production and its cost.

But in Hollywood "nobody knows nothing" . . . and they continue to prove it again and again.

You Forgot to Ask Them What?

Some things are a matter of taste. Others can be considered classics. It takes an almost new level of corporate stupidity to find a way to screw up a product that was both. But never underestimate the power of the modern multinational corporation.

ROBERTO GOIZUETA, CHAIRMAN OF COCA-COLA

UNITED STATES, 1985

Robert Greenberger

Blame Diet Coke. After its successful launch in 1982, the slightly modified no-calorie version of the classic formula was boosting Coca-Cola's revenues, but it was also costing the sugary staple market share. With Pepsi-Cola enjoying a fifteen-year market share increase on one side and Diet Coke (rapidly rising within a year to the number-four soft drink in America) on the other, something had to be done. After all, Coke enjoyed a 60 percent share of the soft drink market immediately after World War II, but by 1983 it was down to just 23 percent. Pepsi was winning where the consumer had a choice, such as supermarkets, while Coke's dominance remained with vending machines and exclusive arrangements at ballparks and fast food franchises.

Coke's stronger aftertaste was losing to Pepsi's sweeter blend as America's taste buds changed over the generations since its introduction in the waning years of the nineteenth century. Dr. John

Pemberton, a pharmacist, came up with the formula at his small drugstore in 1886. He experimented with many flavorings, settling on cola, and yes, it originally had a touch of then-legal cocaine. It was an immediate hit and became popular enough to become one of the first nationwide brands. The original formula, said to be locked in an Atlanta vault, has been unchanged since Pemberton perfected it. The only modification came as a result of economics. For years, Coca-Cola had been slowly introducing the less-expensive high-fructose corn syrup in lieu of cane sugar. By 1980, nearly half the Coke bottled in America contained corn syrup, and by the end of 1984 cane sugar vanished from domestic Coke entirely.

Despite spending $100 million a year on advertising, Coke was still losing to Pepsi. By then, the simple-but-effective Pepsi Challenge was a marketing coup in Pepsi's favor. Roy Stout, head of market research for Coca-Cola USA, said, "If we have twice as many vending machines, dominate fountain, have more shelf space, spend more on advertising, and are competitively priced, why are we losing share? You look at the Pepsi Challenge, and you have to begin asking about taste."

By fall 1983, Sergio Zyman, senior vice president of marketing of Coca-Cola USA, was given the unenviable task of finding a new flavor. The corporate executives spent a year and $4 million trying to find a new flavor for Coke, dubbed Project Kansas, coming up short against Pepsi every time. The research scientists ultimately came up with a hit that tested through the roof, changing the Pepsi Challenge results by eighteen points in Coke's favor. They decided that if people liked the slightly smoother Diet Coke taste, all they had to do was replace the saccharine with corn syrup and a new, improved Coke would exist.

Focus groups with consumers during this time also provided discouraging news. Some said there was no way they'd drink a reformulated Coke. Others said they liked Coke as their favorite drink, but when asked what they actually drank, the answer was all over the map.

People were carefully asked during 200,000 taste tests if they liked the new taste over the old. And while they did prefer the new taste, they also commented that any tampering should not be done to an institution. The focus groups did investigate whether replacing Coca-Cola with New Coke would change their buying habits. Over time, the interpretation was that the switch would cost them 5 to 6 percent of current exclusive buyers. However, the executives presumed these people would be more than made up for by those who liked this new taste over Pepsi or other cola beverages.

Any marketing concerns on changing a classic taste were forgotten in their enthusiasm for the taste test results.

Here was a chance to turn the tables on their chief rival. As a result of that thinking, they chose to retire the current formula in favor of the New Coke. After all, they couldn't market two blends of Coke, since neither one could claim to top Pepsi as America's number-one soft drink. Additionally, when carrying two versions was discussed with their bottlers around the country, it was rejected. At the time, Coca-Cola had expanded their offerings to include Coca-Cola, Diet Coke, Caffeine-Free Diet Coke, Caffeine-Free Coke and Cherry Coke. Plans were already on the boards to introduce Diet Cherry Coke and Minute Maid Orange Soda. The old Coke would have to make way for the New. At corporate headquarters in Atlanta they were elated to see the drink stand up to Pepsi and they were already anticipating the profits.

When the announcement was made, the smiles in the corporate boardroom were replaced with looks of sheer terror. Without even tasting the New Coke, Americans objected to it. After all, Coca-Cola was meddling with something as basic as baseball and apple pie. Its six-ounce curved bottle, descriptive logo lettering and taste harkened back to happier, simpler times and no one wanted to see Coke a victim of corporate greed. For example, when Coca-Cola introduced a ten-ounce bottle in the 1950s, it was soundly rejected by people who disliked the company playing with its identity.

Newspapers editorialized against it; people staged protests, all before a single bottle shipped to the shelves.

On April 23, 1985, the New Coke finally shipped, the same week the old formula was discontinued at bottlers across the country. Critics and consumers alike defied the extensive taste tests marketing had conducted. The new flavor was vilified as "Coke for wimps." While they expected some drop-off in sales to a small segment that preferred the old taste, no one working for the corporation expected outright rejection. While at first the public seemed to accept the new drink, the groundswell against New Coke grew within weeks. This was fanned by newspaper, magazine and television coverage of the rollout. At its peak, Coca-Cola executives blamed the media for turning this into a bigger issue than it should have been. However, that was a miscalculation of the modern age's global village shaping opinion.

Less than two months after its introduction, New Coke was the center of controversy. At corporate headquarters, their consumer hot line was receiving 1,500 calls a day while the negative mail totaled about 40,000 pieces. News organizations happily reported on the formation of groups dedicated to the original formula. The best known were the Old Cola Drinkers of America and Society for the Preservation of the Real Thing.

In his bestselling book on the failure, *The Real Coke, the Real Story*, Thomas Oliver recorded case after case of people rejecting the new blend. One choice example: "There are only two things in my life: God and Coca-Cola. Now you have taken one of those things away from me." Word spread of people hoarding bottles of the old formula, sending for it from Canada or fetching as much as $30 per two-liter bottle on the black market.

Pepsi-Cola USA president Roger Enrico crowed, calling New Coke "the Edsel of the '80s." He noted that Pepsi had successfully built up the notion that their cola drink was for a young, hip Pepsi Generation of consumers. What neither Enrico nor the folks at Coca-Cola counted on was the size of the nostalgia market as the baby boomers, raised on Coke, were beginning to age and think fondly of the past.

Sales plummeted so fast that by July the old formula was announced as making a "triumphant comeback." "We have heard you," said Roberto Goizueta, chairman of Coca-Cola at the time. Donald Keough, president and chief operating officer, added, "The simple fact is that all the time and money and skill poured into consumer research on the new Coca-Cola could not measure or reveal the deep and abiding emotional attachment to original Coca-Cola felt by so many people . . . .

"The passion for original Coca-Cola—and that is the word for it, passion—was something that caught us by surprise . . . It is a wonderful American mystery, a lovely American enigma, and you cannot measure it any more than you can measure love, pride, or patriotism." It may have caught the executives by surprise, but to Joe Public it was a no-brainer.

In retrospect, people thought Coca-Cola goofed and never asked about abandoning the original formula. It has been widely cited as one of the classic marketing blunders of the twentieth century. However, Oliver's book explores the market research and determined where they went wrong. It had more to do with interpreting the data than never asking the key question. Apparently, the misinterpretation of the data occurred in comparing the results of the focus groups with that of a survey conducted using individual interviews with a large representative sample of consumers. There was a conflict in the results between the focus groups and the survey. The survey, it seems, indicated a limited amount of resentment to the abandonment of the original formula compared with the focus groups, which implied this was a much larger bone of contention. Coca-Cola executives followed the conventional rule of thumb that the survey research was more trustworthy than the focus groups'.

Coca-Cola expected some protest, but what surprised them was the vehemence and total sense of alienation the marketing move produced. Everything led them to believe the majority of Coke fans would be bothered to some degree by the change but most would come around.

News of Classic Coca-Cola, as it was dubbed, was important enough for ABC to interrupt afternoon soap operas on July 11 with the announcement. Senator David Pryor of Arkansas called Coke's announcement "a very meaningful moment in the history of America. It shows that some national institutions cannot be changed." Within forty-eight hours of the announcement, the consumer hotline registered 31,600 calls, almost all praising the decision.

By 1986, Classic Coke regained the soft drink crown, defying all marketing expectations at corporate headquarters. New Coke, already renamed Coke II in 1990, was clearly a costly flop, never gaining more than 3 percent of the American market. Interestingly, the company's stock never dipped during the hullabaloo and actually rose after Classic Coke reentered the market. In some ways, the media frenzy helped the company more than a new flavor ever could have. As a result, since the company never really lost any money, the top management team remained in place, whereas in other companies they would have all been replaced in order to save face with Wall Street analysts.

Critics claimed Coke staged the whole thing to mask the introduction of the corn syrup or did it to boost market share. Some went so far as to speculate Coca-Cola was mass-producing Classic Coke all along so they could rush it onto the shelves when New Coke failed. None of these claims have been proven true.

Donald Keough said at the time, "Some critics will say Coca-Cola made a marketing mistake. Some cynics will say that we planned the whole thing. The truth is we are not that dumb, and we are not that smart."

Enrico managed to get his digs in by writing *The Other Guy Blinked*. Using his own hindsight, he wrote, "I think, by the end of their Coca-Cola nightmare, they figured out who they really are. *Caretakers*. They can't change the taste of their flagship brand. They can't change its imagery. All they can do is defend the heritage they nearly abandoned in 1985."

Coca-Cola is smart enough not to avoid the issue of New Coke.

Their Web site has a detailed corporate history, including this questionable chapter. They even have a section where people shared their memories of the change.

On the tenth anniversary of New Coke, an event no one would think was worth remembering, Chairman and Chief Executive Officer Roberto Goizueta used the opportunity to defend "taking intelligent risks." He wanted his staff to feel that taking such risks was necessary. He said, "We set out to change the dynamics of sugar colas in the United States, and we did exactly that—albeit not in the way we had planned . . .the most significant result of 'new Coke'— by far, was that it sent an incredibly powerful signal . . . a signal that we really were ready to do whatever was necessary to build value for the owners of our business."

The speech to employees seemed to avoid the other lesson about messing around with cultural touchstones.

Coke II is still manufactured and sold in selected places around the country but receives no marketing or promotion from Coca-Cola.

INDEX

Perennial

Books by Bill Fawcett:

YOU DID WHAT?
Mad Plans and Great Historical Disasters
ISBN 0-06-053250-5 (paperback)

Kings, corporate leaders, captains, and presidents
throughout history have made horrifically bad
decisions that have had long-lasting effects on the
world. This witty collection chronicles the mayhem committed by the rich and powerful—and even
just the dim-witted—throughout our history.

IT SEEMED LIKE A GOOD IDEA . . .
A Compendium of Great Historical Fiascoes
ISBN 0-380-80771-8 (paperback)
WITH WILLIAM R. FORSTCHEN

Throughout history, the best of intentions—and
sometimes the worst—have resulted in outcomes
vastly different than intended. In this entertaining,
fact-filled volume, explore the moments in history
that began as the best ideas and ended as the
worst fiascoes.